A
Fool
In
Paradise

By
Neil Hutchison

Published by:

Mitraphab Centre Pty Ltd.

Tumbi Umbi, New South Wales, Australia

Cover design and illustrations with the help of

Hans Christian Mueller

Written by:
Neil Hutchison

Other titles by Neil Hutchison:

Money Number One
(A Single Man's Survival Guide to Pattaya)
First Released :   25 December 2001
Reprinted :   14 October 2002
Second Reprint :   24 October 2003

Money Still Number One
(The Single Man's Survival Guide to Thailand)
Due for Release :   April 2004

Acknowledgements

My deep appreciation goes to Alan McEwan for his continued encouragement, support and faith.

I would also like to offer special thanks to my good friend Duncan Stearn for all his help and constructive advice. He graciously consented to edit the final draft so, if there are any typographical errors, grammatical errors or spelling mistakes, it is his fault. Thanks mate.

Thanks also to Hans, Mike and Peter, whose help in getting this book to print was greatly appreciated.

To all the guys who passed on their tales of woe, tales of joy and anecdotes about their Pattaya experiences, keep up the good work. Your story, or part of it, may be included somewhere in the pages that follow but, remember as you read it, some other guy somewhere is reading the same words believing that they were written about him.

Finally, my eternal gratitude to the ladies of Pattaya, even the many who have broken my heart. Without their charm (in winning my heart), smile (as they broke my heart), sense of humour (after breaking my heart) and total unpredictability (I never saw it coming), the Pattaya story for me would be a one line entry in some obscure travel guide to South East Asia.

About This Book

What follows is a collection of observations, personal opinions and experience. The stories are all true except for the ones that aren't. These could best be described as being 'based on true events'. Most names have been changed to protect the innocent or stupid. Names of the guilty have not been changed because they are the bastards I want to get.

Many of the stories were first published in *Pattaya Expat* magazine, *Pattaya Trader* magazine and *Pattaya Today* newspaper.

The chapters fall in no particular order but, where two or more tales are related, they should appear in more or less chronological order.

The last chapter, 'Footprints in the Sand', is different. It is not meant to be amusing, but was written as the events unfolded. It needed to be written and needs to be read by anyone who believes that Pattaya will not or can not affect their lives. It needs to be read by any man currently in a relationship or contemplating entering a relationship with a Thai lady. The story is not unique by any means, but demonstrates how little we actually know about ourselves and how little we foreign men understand about the nature of Thai women.

Contents

1

Introduction

There have been so many words already penned about Pattaya –
that place on the eastern seaboard of Thailand variously described
as Thailand's Premier Beach Resort, Fun Town, Sin City or The
Sex Capital of Asia. Search the Internet and you will soon realize that
the human life span is too short to read everything written in cyberspace
about this unique city.

The popularity of the place cannot be denied. According to Tourism
Authority of Thailand figures, in 2001 Pattaya received a total of 3.86
million visitors staying an average of 4.33 days and spending an average
of 3,016 *baht* (about US$75) per person per day. This contributed a
total of about 32.72 billion *baht* (US$815 million) to the Thai economy.

Nobody will ever convince me that the majority of the Western male
tourists travel thousands of kilometres to see temples, buy copy t-shirts,
play golf or go scuba diving. Personally, I already have a wardrobe full
of copy shirts and, once I've seen one temple, I figure that I've seen
them all. I don't play golf because I have a handicap - I cannot hit the
ball. On the rare occasion that I do actually hit it, it never goes where I
want it to. I also accept that the only creatures equipped to safely
investigate the underwater world are fish. The only remaining attractions
are the bars and the nocturnal entertainment scene so it follows that
these must be a major draw card for others as well as myself.

Pattaya is such an interesting place. Nothing is black and white here. It is all grey, from the complex legal system down to the day to day selective reasoning of the people. Winston Churchill, in October 1939, described Russia as "a riddle wrapped in a mystery inside an enigma." The great man may or may not have been right about Russia but, if he was talking about Thailand, he would certainly have been correct.

It is not the countryside, the city, the beaches or the scenery, but the people who are the real asset. There are better cities, cleaner beaches and more picturesque scenery elsewhere in Thailand but the people of Pattaya capture your heart and curiosity. Within the space of five minutes you can meet a person who believes you should give him or her twenty *baht* simply because you are a foreigner, then meet someone who will offer to share the meal they just purchased with their last twenty *baht*. In this city of immigrants and transients from all across Thailand and every corner of the globe, money is both cross-cultural and multilingual. Show me a place in the world where it isn't.

As it is with most people, I like humour and enjoy anything that makes me laugh. In Pattaya, humour can emanate from the most unlikely sources. I am also a student of and unfortunately, a prime example of, human stupidity. It never ceases to amaze me that the human race has developed the technology to transport a man to Mars and we can now successfully transplant almost every major organ in the human body, yet we are capable of the most idiotic acts.

> *"You know how dumb the average person is? Well, by definition, half of them are dumber than that."*
> Rev. J.R. "Bob" Dobbs
> Church of the Sub-Genius

Foreign visitors to the Land of Smiles are not noted for their displays of common sense, so uncovering amusing stories about their misadventures is not difficult. There is no shortage of material around, beginning with the guy who, in an act of alcohol-assisted stupidity, gave a motorcycle taxi driver a US$100 note, instructing him to go to a currency exchange office, change it for *baht* and bring the money back to the bar he was drinking at. And he wasn't a tourist - he was a long-term resident! Brain cell in overdrive.

Yes, the bar scene plays an important role and is a veritable gold mine of tales. The primal story is played out daily in the *sois*. For 'Garden of Eden' read 'Pattaya', for 'Eve' read 'bar girl' and for 'apple' read 'sick buffalo story'. The snake can be interpreted as that dangly bit between a man's legs and for 'Adam' read 'foreign male'. Each time Eve presents Adam with her apple, he happily swallows it and wanders off into the night with Eve and his snake.

Holidaymakers, even if it is not their first time, tend to get caught up in the hedonistic lifestyle. On their day of departure, they ask themselves two questions: "How did I end up spending so much money?" and "How soon can I get back here?" Those coming to start a business or to retire, having already gone through the overindulgent holiday routine, progress through other definitive stages.

Initially, they try to fight against the system. They judge the place by Western standards and try to understand it from that perspective. They try to change their new environment to suit how they were brought up and taught to do things. Those entrepreneurs setting up businesses soon discover why all the signposts on the road to poverty are written in Thai.

Once they realize they are not going to change anything, the second stage is to become bitter and cynical. They realize they cannot live like a tourist every day but, in doing so, no longer trust anyone and life becomes a trial supplemented by copious amounts of giggle-juice to ease the pain. Many more falter at this point.

The third stage is acceptance. They go native, go with the flow and do not let too many things upset them. They learn to enjoy the enjoyable, adapt to the adaptable, endure the unfortunate times and pass off any disappointments as just part of the learning curve. They realize that Pattaya is a game and, if you play it wisely, everybody wins.

For some of us there is a fourth and final stage. We write about it. Pattaya is to a writer what a room full of fruit bowls is to an artist. There is an adventure around every corner and a story in every person we meet. We write about the incredulous events that make everyday life here surreal and do it with the knowledge that much of what we write will not be believed by the outside world.

The difficulty, for me, was how to write the tales. The consequences of many foreigner's follies are relatively benign but, as an objective observer, it would be difficult to make the stories amusing without sounding condescending or belittling the hapless character. Even though we all like to laugh at ourselves and many Western jokes centre around someone else's misfortune, the poor sod reading his own tale made frivolous by someone who was not involved, may not find it so amusing.

The point I hope to get across in all my writing is that I love Pattaya. I love the town itself, the people and the whole lifestyle. Sure I complain about the place at times and at times I am critical and cynical, at times morose and sometimes even angry or bitter. But in spite of all its shortcomings, in spite of the many frustrations and the occasional heartbreaks, Pattaya is exciting.

Telling a friend in Australia about my adventures in Thailand, his wife soberly remarked that I was a fool living in a fool's paradise and I should return to the 'real' world. At the time I laughed it off, but what she said did bear thinking about. It is true I consider Thailand to be a paradise and it is also true that the place can be deceptive from time to time. Would I prefer to live in a fool's paradise or a wise man's purgatory? Even saying the word 'purgatory' sends shivers down my spine and since I have never considered myself to be 'wise', the question was similar to asking whether I would prefer to make love with Miss Universe or have a molten lead enema. So, here I am, a not so wise man living in a deceptively wonderful place - a fool in paradise. Furthermore, it is *my* paradise and the only place I call home.

2

Early Retirement

I retired at age forty. There was no particular justification for it, I simply wanted to. I came to the conclusion that I no longer believed in organized work (not that I ever really did) and, just as I had with organized religion before it, decided to give it the big flick.

My parents would have turned in their graves with the knowledge that I had not listened to anything they tried to teach me. Their attempts to install some form of work ethic in me fell on deaf ears. According to them, after getting a good education, I was supposed to work hard, raise a family, work even harder, deprive myself, act with restraint and eventually succeed in owning a scrap of dirt with a pile of sticks on it. Then, I had to keep doing the same thing for another quarter century and put aside money for my old age.

For what? So that I could be old, feeble and rich? Being slouched in a wheelchair, dribbling my breakfast gruel while having a million dollars in the bank is not my idea of fun. I could never imagine myself sitting there being spoon-fed by some sour-faced nurse and thinking what I would like to do with her but not being able to remember exactly what that was.

I was born the black sheep of the family. My elder brother always said that the first word I spoke was not 'mama', but 'baaa'. In the

14

succeeding years, I failed miserably at living up to the family motto - 'Work will make you free' - because I always perceived pleasure as a much more sensible idea than pain and play as infinitely better than work. Not that I'm lazy, mind you, I just don't see the point.

Maybe it is because I am the only member of my extended and confused bloodline to have never fought in a war. The Korean conflictwas a done deal before I was even born and the Vietnam debacle was over before I reached the legal age to kill people. My father, mother, brother and all my uncles and aunts fought in war. My grandparents actually started one. Winston Churchill said, "there is nothing more exhilarating than to be shot at without result." Perhaps therein lies my problem but I am in no hurry to test Sir Winston's theory.

Maybe it is because I am an atheist. I believe in evolution and the consequences of random events. I don't believe in an afterlife or a past life or in any superior being apart from Mother Nature herself. She is the one who made us and, when she has had enough giggles, she will get rid of us. Therefore, I believe in life and life is the here and now. Learn from the past, plan for the future and live for the present.

Sounds good, doesn't it? All except for three things. Firstly, it seems that every time I planned for the future, the future had different plans for me. Thinking any more than twenty-four hours ahead was merely setting myself up for disappointment. Secondly, experience has taught me that I learn from past mistakes only after I have repeated them - several times - just to make sure. Thirdly, I am not that good at living for the present. I am 'here', it is 'now', but without adequate funds, I am living a quality of life nowhere near that to which I should become accustomed. Basically, I am living by the seat of my pants.

Maybe it is because my life has been devoid of heroes. My father died before I was old enough to appreciate him and I was left with my workaholic brother as my only role model. I love him dearly but he was cast from a different mould in that he has been nauseatingly successful at anything and everything he has attempted. I became tired of trying to live up to his example so I simply stopped trying.

If I had one hero it would be Sir Isaac Newton, in my opinion the greatest genius that randomly-merged atoms have produced. He is credited with inventing calculus. Invented it? I could not understand it even when it was explained to me by people who had pictures to prove that it worked! He also came up with some universal laws of nature. I particularly enjoy his First Law of Motion. This states that, "every body continues in its state of rest ... unless it is compelled to change that state by forces impressed upon it." Shit, I could have told him that.

By age thirty-nine, I had been through the marriage, mortgage and two point three children bit (in my case I rounded it up to three), and decided that nothing would be served by me remaining another brick in the wall. I would stand aside and let a younger person take my place in the system.

At forty, I figured that, since I was still physically healthy and mentally suspect, I wanted to enjoy the rest of my life. Luckily, fate then stepped in and allowed me the privilege of experiencing the 'divorce' and 'penniless' stages of the normal life process. This was the turning point and, with nothing left to lose, I realized that lack of assets was just one less burden I had to carry. I calculated that I was past the halfway point in my life and observed that material wealth was no good to a person once they're dead. Therefore, if I couldn't take it with me, I didn't want it.

My own government did not take my decision as well as I had expected. I tried to explain to the brain-dead, pencil-pusher behind the desk that I had voluntarily chosen early retirement. Could I please get my pension early? If I thought he displayed a remarkable sense of humour then, what really cracked him up was when I informed him of my plan to move to Thailand and asked that it be paid to me in *baht*. I didn't wait for his answer.

The Thai Government representative at the Embassy smiled and said I was too young to retire and without an Australian pension coming in, I was merely a 'low-class' tourist that Thailand could do without. Flattery gets you nowhere. He then offered to show me a photograph of a Thai temple, laughing that it was as close as I was ever likely to get to one.

16

As it turns out, after having now lived in Thailand for almost five years, he was right.

What was wrong with my idea? I would have thought that my government would be pleased to see the last of someone they had always treated as a blot on Australia's sunburnt landscape. I would be happy living out my final years in Thailand and the Thai government should be happy with the foreign income I brought into the country. Win, win, win. Alas, it appeared nobody but me could see the big picture.

Undaunted, I went ahead with implementing the 'retire in a foreign country' plan which consisted of simply that - the title. Never having reached the stage of actually working out the finer details of how I was going to achieve this miracle of survival, I decided to wing it. And, in hindsight, living from day-to-day is probably the best way to proceed in Thailand. Here, laws and opinions change faster than the wind direction so having a security blanket today is no guarantee of stability or permanence.

So it's now and I'm here. Plan A. I have officially retired from the workforce and effectively retired from the human race. In case Thailand refuses to cooperate, I have Plan B which involves a small travel bag of essentials and a plane ticket at the travel agency waiting for me to raise the funds to pay for it. If I further suspect there may be uniformed, official-looking people waiting for me at Australia's entry points with a pressing desire to 'talk' to me (that's another story), I also have Plan C.

This involves an overland route out of Thailand to Phnom Penh where I intend to throw myself at the mercy of the Cambodian people and be either granted asylum or admitted to one.

3

Advanced
Watchmaking

I was on a flight from the Philippines to Australia after having spent a few days in Manila visiting my brother and his family. With my twelve-month valid return air ticket about to expire, it was time for my annual pilgrimage to Brisbane. I usually stay about a week which gives me plenty of time to visit my children, who I love dearly, catch up with some old friends and check that my bank accounts have not been closed in my absence at the request of the bank's Credit Department. A visit to the Thai Embassy for a new visa is also on the itinerary. The whole process usually takes three working days but, to be perfectly honest, from the moment I set foot back in Australia I can not wait to leave the place. I stay for a week merely to keep up appearances.

Due to my late arrival at Manila airport check-in, I was squeezed into one of the most uncomfortable of the economy class seats. Standard punishment for late arrival is to be given no choice of seating. This particular airline had gone to the extra trouble of making all the economy seats an inch or two narrower so they could cram more people in. The other passengers were obviously fully aware that my particular seat was the worst on the aircraft and I was sure I could hear the sniggering as I adjusted my seatbelt. "That'll teach him to be late!" I won't mention the name of the airline because I may have to travel with them again and I don't fancy sitting on the wing, even though, after six hours in my seat, the wing began to look somewhat appealing.

18

It happened as I was making the two-hour time adjustment on my wristwatch. The pin holding the band to the face of the watch snapped. This was of no major concern, merely annoying. My watch has a gold-plated metal band with four pins holding it all together. I've had it for two years and it seems that the pins, made of some highly corrosive metal, take it in turns to break. Living in the heat and humidity of South East Asia, my sweat must take on toxic properties with devastating effect. Two years, six pins. Not a real problem. Easy to fix. I placed the watch in my top pocket and went back to squirming in my seat.

My time in Australia was busier than I had anticipated. I visited my children, went to see my bank - no photo of me on the wall, always a good sign. Paid a few bills. The usual stuff. The following Friday I was ready and keen to leave so made my way into the city to pick up my return ticket to Bangkok, having collected my new Thai visa the previous day.

With the airline ticket tucked safely in my pocket, I stopped for a quiet lunch. It was only when someone asked me for the time that I remembered to get my watch fixed. I had never needed to have my watch repaired in Australia before but since I was in the heart of Brisbane City, it seemed an appropriate place. There were several watchmakers and jewellers about. First stop was the biggest name jeweller in Brisbane.

"Can I help you sir?"

"Yes. The pin in my watch-band has broken and I need a replacement."

"Oh, sorry sir, we can't do it today. Our watchmaker is off sick. Can you bring it back tomorrow?"

"No, I can't come back tomorrow. It is only a simple job, isn't there anyone else who can do it?"

"No sir. We leave that to our professionals."

"Thanks."

Fifty metres down the mall was another big name jewellery store. With no other customers about, it should not take too long.

"Certainly sir. We can fix it for you. Leave it with us and you can pick it up tomorrow afternoon after four o'clock."

"I can't pick it up tomorrow. I'm leaving the country at eleven in the morning. It's not a big job, can't you do it now?"

"No sir. This watch requires a special pin and we don't have one in stock. Can't do it today."

I had long suspected that the pins in my watch band were special and now it had been confirmed. The biodegradable non-rustproof metal was probably imported from the US. My guess was that it was developed in some top-secret laboratory during the Cold War with the plan to sneak it into Russian armaments factories to ensure that their weapons would disintegrate the first time they were fired. There was another watchmaker across the street so I decided on one last try.

"Yes sir, not a problem. Leave it here and it will be ready tomorrow morning after nine."

"But it is only a simple job. I need it now."

"Oh, no sir. It requires a special pin."

Again with the 'special pin' bit.

"Why is it so special? It is just an ordinary watch."

"Where did you buy it, sir?"

"In Hong Kong. It was only one of twenty thousand I had to choose from."

"Aaaaaaah. I see." The condescending 'you're a Cheap Charlie' look on his face said it all as he handed me back the watch.

"Ok, so if I pick it up tomorrow morning, how much will it be?"

"Twenty-five dollars, sir."

"Goodbye."

At that point, there was no alternative but to wait until I got to Thailand to see if anyone there could repair the special watch that three professionals in Australia could not.

The flight to Bangkok was uneventful. Different airline, better seat, same inedible food. Through Immigration and Customs without a hitch and, since I do not enjoy hanging around airports or Bangkok for that matter, I booked a taxi to take me straight to Pattaya. It was the perfect opportunity to get some shuteye on the way because I find it impossible to sleep on airplanes and, unless you are the driver, it is too frightening to watch the road ahead while driving in Thailand. I woke up just as we reached the hotel.

It was eight o'clock by the time I finished unpacking and drowning myself under a nice warm shower. I decided to go out to visit some of my friends and have a soothing cold ale to ward off jetlag and berri berri. Crossing Pattaya Central Road, I noticed a lady sitting on a plastic stool behind a wooden bench. A glass case on the bench proudly displayed a diverse array of watch bands, locks and keys. Taking my watch from my pocket (I was getting quite used to it being in my pocket by now and treated it as my very own fob watch), I handed it to the lady asking, in bamboo English, "You can fix?"

With a nod of her head she laid the watch on the bench then took out a petite hammer and a thin nail-like object. A tap-tap here, a crimp there, and it was done. Four minutes later she handed me the repaired article.
"How much?" I asked.
"Twenty *baht*," she replied, looking rather apologetic.

As if I cared. I would have paid her 200 *baht* I was so grateful. No "come back tomorrow" or "special pin" arguments. This lovely lady, using rudimentary equipment, did in four minutes and for ninety Australian cents, what the three biggest jewellers in Brisbane could not do in less than twenty-four hours and for under twenty-five dollars. And they have the hide to call Thailand a third world country.

4

Buffalo River

Firstly, I should point out that I am a normal, everyday, run-of-the-mill type person. Like every other average, nondescript person on this planet, I maintain a list of people who, for a variety of valid reasons, I wish to kill. The list is continually amended and updated and contains names such as my bank manager, his credit officer and the guy who, in 1990, told me "Don't go to Thailand. There is nothing there worth seeing." It also contains groups of people for whom I can find no redeeming qualities. These include politicians (naturally enough), taxi drivers and those movie sound technicians who insist on maintaining all dialogue at a whisper while the action scenes and music soundtrack are at such a decibel level that it blows the viewer of his couch.

About a year ago it became necessary to add yet another low-life to my list. Luckily for him, I don't know his name, but he probably had something to do with the classic movie *Bridge on the River Kwai*. His crime is that he is the one who decided to pronounce the name of this now famous river to rhyme with 'my' and 'shy'. The actors in the movie followed this idiot's direction and since then, every English-speaking person I know has pronounced it the same way.

On my third trip to Pattaya, I decided to get away from the rigours of bar life for one or two days and do something 'touristy'. A visit to a site of historical importance, especially to the English and Australians, was just what the doctor ordered. That way, in years to come, when my grandchildren ask "What did you do in Thailand, Granddad?", I don't have to answer, "I sat at a bar every night, drinking beer."

I mentioned my desire to visit the River Kwai to my girlfriend.
"You want to see buffalo?"
It was then that I remembered that '*Kwai*' was the Thai word for 'buffalo'.
"We go *Chonburi*. Have buffalo too much."
No, I do not want to see buffalo. I then came to the erroneous conclusion that the River *Kwai* was probably 'Buffalo River' in English. A different tactic was called for.
"*Nahm*," I stated, making snake-like motions with my hand in a childish attempt to mimic a flowing river. I knew the word for 'water' because I add a little of the stuff to my scotch. (Who said that you never learn anything sitting in a bar all night?)
"*Nahm Kwai*," was my next attempt. "A very famous place."

The blank look on her face meant that I was still not getting my message across.
"You want give buffalo water?"
With that, I dived into my suitcase for my Thai-English phrasebook.
"*Mair-nahm Kwai*," I joyfully exclaimed, having found the translation for 'river'.
"River Buffalo?" she inquired.
"Yes! Yes! That's it."
"*Mai roo-juk*."
Back to the phrasebook.
"What do you mean you don't know it? You must have heard of it. It's very famous."
"*Mai roo-juk*."

It was then that I decided to take a break. We were both getting too frustrated at our communication breakdown. I concluded that the love of my life was either a sandwich short of a picnic or not very well traveled in Thailand.

For the next two days, I mentioned my quest to everyone who would listen. Every foreigner I spoke to knew exactly what I was talking about, whereas every Thai looked at me as if I was from Mars. '*Mair-nahm Kwai*' just did not register with them. I even went to see a Thai lady that I have known since my very first trip to Pattaya. She is a dear friend and speaks English very well. "River Buffalo? *Mai roo-juk*," came the now-familiar response.

It was at this point that paranoia stepped in. Obviously, there was a secret code that I was missing. Every Thai knew it, but they have all been sworn never to divulge it to me. Maybe it was the tone? I then proceeded to pronounce '*Kwai*' in each of the five tones of the Thai language. Everyone within earshot must have thought I was practising for the Vienna Choir, or at least, a karaoke night. Their amusement at my verbal antics left me in no doubt that I was still on the wrong track.

The moment of salvation came on the third day when my angel and I walked past a travel agency with an advertisement for day trips to 'The River *Kwai*' in the window. The ad was written in both English and Thai. As if I had just found the Holy Grail, I joyfully pointed to the ad exclaiming, "There! There! That's where I want to go!"

"*Mair-nahm Kwair*? *Kanchanaburi*. Very beautiful," she proudly retorted with the confidence of a TAT travel guide. At this point, the penny dropped.

"*Kwair*? *Kwair*?" My voice was starting to reach fever pitch.

"You mean that all this time I have been pronouncing the word '*Kwai*' as it is written, when in fact, it should be pronounced 'K-W-A-I-R' to rhyme with 'air' and 'share'?"

My delicate flower did not understand this last question, however two hundred metres down the road, the foreign tourists who heard me understood perfectly. Jubilation turned to anger and then to outright hatred for the son-of-a-*kwai* who decided to anglicize the Thai name for the river to '*Kwai*' and not '*Kwair*'.

With my lady smiling brightly, her pearly-whites sparkling in the sunlight and her eyes positively glowing at the thought of a free holiday up country to beautiful *Kanchanaburi*, I spat the dummy, gloomily proclaiming, "I don't want to go now."

Thankfully for the human race, time heals all wounds. Nevertheless, it took three days for my anger over the *kwai/kwair* episode to subside. That, plus constant nagging from my heart-throb who made it her life's mission to keep reminding me of my 'promise' to take her to *Kanchanaburi*. I could not recall making such a promise, but one of the unfortunate consequences of getting drunk from time to time is that you just never know, do you?

Anyway, late one night when I was at my most vulnerable, I agreed that we would go to the River Kwair. How will we get there? The little extortionist beside me was a fountain of knowledge.

"Car. You rent car. Man can drive. Go *ray-o ray-o*. *Pun hah baht. Mai pairng*."

My Thai language skills went into a tailspin. Being totally inept, I wondered how she came up with the exact figure of 1,005 *baht*. That was my first mistake. The second came a few minutes later.

My charming companion asked, "I bring friend, Ok?" Because I am such a nice guy, I felt it would be good if she brought a friend along. Her English was as pitiful as my Thai, so it would be convenient to have someone for her to talk with along the way. Plenty of room in the car. If you are an expat or have been in Thailand for more than a week, you will be smiling right now because you know exactly what happened next.

Early the following morning, I rented a car plus driver at 1,500 *baht* for the day. End of Thai Language lesson number one. We then drove to another part of Pattaya to pick up her 'friend'. After receiving somewhat vague directions from my sweetheart, the driver pulled up in front of an out-of-the-way apartment building. Lesson number two is that there are no plurals in the Thai language. When she asked if she could bring a 'friend' along, she really meant 'friends'. One toot of the horn and out popped two delightful young ladies, eagerly skipping towards the car with strides as wide as their respective smiles. As their smiles grew larger, mine grew smaller. A bit of quick banter, then the three of them eased into the back seat. I was relegated to the front, where I would learn another valuable lesson over the next ten hours. In Thailand, unless you are the driver, never sit in a vehicle where you get a full, unobstructed view of the road ahead. I aged ten years that day.

Don't think it ended there. No, no, no. As we squeezed out of the small *soi* back to the paved road, who should we see but another old friend who had no plans for the day. The conversation, when loosely translated to English, went something like this:

Long Lost Friend:	"Where are you going?"
Girlfriend:	"*Kanchanaburi.*"
Long Lost Friend:	"Can I come?"
Girlfriend:	"Sure. Get in."

Formalities completed, the three freeloaders took over the back seat and my lady-love sat on my lap in the front.

You might say that, except for supplying a well-padded cushion, I took no further part in the activities in the vehicle. With my girlfriend sitting on my lap, her head and body twisted towards the rear seat containing her three 'bestest' friends, the conversation was nonstop to *Kanchanaburi*. I now have a 20% hearing loss in my right ear due to the incessant cackling directly beside my head. This hearing loss aside, the forward journey was uneventful. My eyes were closed.

Upon arrival, the first priority was, of course, to eat. Actually, my first priority was to get the blood re-circulating through my paralysed legs. My heart had been advertising in the *Bangkok Post* 'Lost Property' column for the missing arteries in my legs. The selection of restaurant was left up to the girls. There were only one hundred or so eating establishments to choose from, all equally good, but the girls needed to check out at least half of them before making such an important decision. Finally, they led the driver and me to a suitable place whereupon I recorded my first victory on Thai soil.

Their eagerness to get me to sit down set off alarm bells in my head. I explained that I was not really hungry (true) and that I would have a walk around instead. The four girls then set upon me, literally dragging me to the table. This made me even more determined to resist and my protest finally succeeded. I walked away to the sound of some very frantic Thai conversation.

Forty minutes later I wandered back to a camouflaged position from which I could observe the restaurant. The quintet finally left the table, the driver returning to the car and the ladies appearing as if they were about to split up into search parties to retrieve me. I casually made my way towards the car and a cool reception from my girlfriend. I knew, by her look, that my plan was a success. If I had sat at the table with them, even if I only ate a spoonful of rice, I would have been liable for the entire bill. By my absence, the bill was left to them. It was a shallow victory, because my girlfriend ended up paying and guess where she got the money? It doesn't matter. Shallow victory or not, I will take what I can get.

We continued our journey to the River *Kwair*. The place was beautiful, interesting and historic but, being somewhat jaded, a river is a river and frankly, when you have seen one bridge, you have seen them all. I was saddened to learn that the original structure built by the POWs was not destroyed in the manner depicted in the movie. Rather unromantically, it was simply bombed from the air. We walked across the restored bridge, bought some souvenirs and took some photos.

The return trip was quite different because my lady and the three freeloaders slept the entire way. Not a peep out of any of them. Although my right ear was saved from further torture, my legs were again treated to a holiday from fresh blood supply and my stress level rose in proportion to the amount of time I watched the road and traffic ahead. Safely back in the sanity of Pattaya, after disgorging Curly, Larry and Mo, I paid off the driver (including a substantial tip for some innovative driving techniques) and proceeded to the hotel. Later that evening, sitting alone at my favourite bar, my lady-love sound asleep in our room after such an exhausting day, I decided to return to the River *Kwair* some day. Next time though, I will go unaided, unescorted and therefore unstressed.

5

Security
Consciousness

They say a man's home is his castle. If this is true then I must live in the dungeon. My home, or should I say apartment, is not only primitive by Western standards, it is primitive by anyone's standards. The lacklustre accommodation consists of a small room with four walls surrounding an even smaller room with two walls. This small room consists of a hole in the floor through which everything passes and a hole in the wall through which hopefully water passes. I have a nagging concern that the hole in the floor of the apartment above is somehow connected to the hole in the wall of my apartment. Suffice to say if I was the real estate agent empowered with selling the benefits of owning or renting this Shangri La, it would be difficult to describe all the features to potential customers, simply because there are none. It is featureless, tasteless, comfortless and hopeless.

The reason that I chose to live in such a dour setting is easier to explain - money. With all its negative attributes it does have one major asset - it is cheap. I calculated that until such time as I become extremely wealthy, something that I'm sure will happen any day now, I have to live as economically as possible. If this means forgoing some of life's little luxuries, then so be it.

In any case, my cell is full of ecology. I get all four seasons in the one room - it is hot when the weather outside is hot, it is wet when it rains, it is insect-infested in the spring and, when the fan works, it is humid and sticky. Everything that a whale-saving tree-worshipping greeny like me could want.

The apartment building itself consists of four floors with three cells to each floor. Several months ago we had a major problem. Within the space of three days the apartments either side of mine were broken into. One had the TV, video and stereo system stolen while the other had the TV and some jewellery taken. Both tenants were furious and I'm sure they were casting accusing eyes in my direction since my place was untouched. In an effort to stifle gossip and set their minds at ease, we met as a group and I showed them my room. Both were very apologetic as they assumed that I had indeed also been robbed. I was forced to confess that what little possessions they saw were in fact what little possessions I owned.

The group then checked the locks on our respective doors to find that my lock was different from theirs. One of them locked his door from the inside then produced a screwdriver and proceeded to open it again by simply turning the screwdriver in the lock. The same happened with the other apartment, whereas, given the same treatment, my own lock remained secure. The reason for the thief's lack of interest in my apartment was now obvious. The fitted locks were only for show and would deter none but the laziest of thieves.

The manager of the building was dragged kicking and screaming into the midst of our concerns and made aware of the shortcomings in the security area. He agreed to install large metal plates to each door so that we could padlock it ourselves. He further explained that the building already had a security grille on the front, and only, entrance and that only the tenants were given a key. We should always ensure that the grille remained locked. I thought that he had raised a valid point. That is until I went out to see if I could get a copy of the security key cut so I would have a spare. I thought there could be a problem having a security key copied, as is the case in my home country. Imagine my surprise when the little key-cutting man on the plastic stool took one look at my key and handed me a perfect replica straight off the rack.

Twenty *baht*. Any potential thief in Pattaya could have done the same so, as a first line of defence, the security gate rated a mere twenty *baht*.

True to the manager's word, the next day large hardened steel plates were attached to the door and the door jamb with a large hole cut through each to fit our padlocks. Several thieves with sharp hacksaws and working in shifts would take a week to cut their way through these suckers. I immediately went out and purchased the biggest mother of a padlock I could lay my hands on. I gave a copy of the padlock key and the security key to my live-in temporary girlfriend (she refers to herself as my 'wife') and felt sure that all precautions were now in place.

A week later I returned to my room late in the afternoon and my heart sank when I noticed the door ajar as I approached. I had definitely locked it before I ventured out. My heart sank further when I noticed that the massive padlock was still in place but the bulletproof steel plate on the door had been ripped from the timber. My heart sank even further when I pushed the door open to find my girlfriend lying on the bed. "What the f—?"

To cut a long story short, it appeared that, when she left for work earlier in the morning (yes, I do let her work, not so much for the money as for the twelve hours of peace and quiet it affords me), she had forgotten to take her keys. Some hours later she developed a severe stomach ache and a desperate need to go back to the room. She borrowed the manager's duplicate key to open the door lock. As he did not have a copy of the key to the padlock, she then used her forty-five kilo frame behind a swift kick to smash her way in.

I wondered what the penalty was in Thailand for justifiable homicide. My fury at her subsided once I checked the damage to the door. The nuclear weapon proof plate had been attached to the hollow plywood door with five half-inch wood screws. The attachment was so fragile even a child could have pushed it open. So much for security measure number two. I repaired the door as best I could and hoped that the mere size of the padlock would act as a deterrent. Again, it would only discourage an honest, lazy or stupid thief.

For a time after that episode, things ran smoothly in Apartment Alcatraz. There were no reported burglaries in the other units and my own non-childproof door was holding fast. Every morning my little limpet mine would toddle off to work and I would enjoy several more hours of blissful sleep.

On one such occasion I awoke from my late morning nap with the unnerving feeling that I was not alone. I was sleeping on my side with my back to the door but could sense movement in the room behind me. It is bad enough waking from a dream involving a sexual marathon with several famous Hollywood actresses, but to turn over and find a strange woman standing in the middle of your room is truly a heart starter.

"Who the hell are you?" was all I could say.

She was young, attractive, well-dressed and appeared a little shocked that she had woken me. From where she was standing, I guessed she had been giving the room the once-over looking for cash or anything of value lying around. She had already opened the solitary cupboard and was preparing to open the only drawer. Startled, she *wai*-ed, uttered something in Thai, backed towards the door and made a swift exit. I thought about chasing her but decided against it due to the fact I was stark naked. My clothes were all hanging in the wardrobe and my towel was wherever my soon-to-be-strangled girlfriend, who never locked the door on her way out, threw it. I concluded that the sight of a naked *fa-lung* chasing a young Thai girl down the street may raise a few eyebrows and require a lot of explaining should it attract the attention of the local police.

On a positive note, her intrusion did provide me with some degree of satisfaction. I pictured her vaulting down the stairs to her waiting boyfriend on the getaway motorcycle and telling him that "apartment floor three have nothing worth taking." I finally had the ultimate security system.

6

Reality Check

I have to confess something, but if you ever repeat it I will deny that I ever said it. I'm a fraud, a fake, as phony as the Rolex timepieces sold on the streets of Bangkok. A one hundred percent copy *fa-lung*. I am a man who has lived in Pattaya long enough to know better. A man who has written a book about the bar girls of Pattaya. Someone who, although never professing to be an expert on any subject, by the mere fact of giving advice to other *fa-lung*, has implied some degree of knowledge about the bar scene. Now I had broken my own cardinal rule. I had let one of the little darlings get to me.

It all began one night when I was out wandering the streets looking for anything new or interesting. I literally stumbled across a beer bar that had newly opened. It looked squeaky clean, the girls were attractive and, more importantly, there was no other *fa-lung* about. It was inviting enough to pop in for at least one drink to check it out.

Six hours later, my jaw was aching from laughing so much, my head was spinning from drinking so much, my legs were aching from dancing, I had 'rung the bell' twice, was having the time of my life and still I was the only *fa-lung* at the bar. The girls were attentive, fun-loving, not pushy and all new to Pattaya. Not once was I asked to play one of those stupid bar games. If Pattaya is heaven on earth then I had discovered heaven's heaven. One girl in particular caught my eye.

During the next few weeks I frequented the bar almost every evening. The *mamasan* spoke reasonable English and was appreciative of my patronage. To be more accurate, she enjoyed the patronage of my holidaying free-spending *fa-lung* friends that I would bring along to the bar. Every time one of my friends came to town I would introduce him around and each one agreed that this bar was better than the run-of-the-mill beer bar. I was hooked and could not get enough of it. I continued paying special attention to the girl who had initially attracted me, buying her drinks and calling her my *tee-ruk*. The other girls understood that, if ever I was going to bar fine one of them, it would be her.

One piece of my own advice that I do follow is that, if ever I enjoy drinking and socializing at a particular bar, I never rush in and bar fine one of the girls too early. Eventually you will break up with her or want to go with another of the girls from the bar. It is a sure way of getting someone off side and ending what could have been a long and pleasant relationship. The tension and back-stabbing that follows makes it very uncomfortable to return for a relaxing evening. My other reason is that, er, well, at the time I was already attached as it were and living with my 'Thai wife'. I know I have already confessed to being a fraud, but I may have failed to mention hypocrisy. Another of my personality disorders.

The rot set in one evening at the bar while I was drinking with a friend and having a great time as usual. I had bought my *tee-ruk* a couple of drinks, was holding her hand and did not notice two Dutchmen arrive and sit at the other end of the bar. My *tee-ruk* quietly got up from the stool beside me and proceeded back behind the bar to serve them their drinks. At least, that is what I thought. I paid little attention and had my back turned to the new customers.

Moments later there was chatter among the other girls, so I turned around to behold my *tee-ruk* holding hands with one of the Dutchmen and receiving a tonsillectomy from his tongue. I hate to admit it, but my heart sank. This was the girl who would turn her head to the side whenever I went to kiss her on the lips. This was the girl who was so shy that she became noticeably embarrassed each time I hugged her in public. The same one who told me she loved me. This was the girl who had not even finished the last fucking 'lady drink' I had bought for her!

Reality check. This is Pattaya. This is fantasyland. Nothing is real. The amount of true love to be found in the collective hearts of the bar girls of Pattaya could be carried on the back of one crippled ant while the amount of bullshit would fertilize the Sahara. I know this just as I know that the sun will rise in the east tomorrow. I also know most people would think that it served me right, she is a working girl and since the money did not seem to be forthcoming from me, it has to come from somewhere. I was too slow and should have paid her bar fine much earlier. I should not be angry with her for doing her job. And they are correct. But I was not so much angry at her as I was with myself for letting it affect me. I thought the years had rendered me immune to all that.

Personally I do not have any problem with the bar girls, even the ones I like and those who profess to like me, going off with as many other *fa-lung* as they can. It is their job, pure and simple. Experienced bar girls are usually very adept at juggling boyfriends around and I never get jealous or angry. If my *tee-ruk* was not at work one evening and I was told that she had gone with another customer or if I arrived late at the bar to find her already with another customer, I would think nothing of it. It is however considered very bad form to change from one *fa-lung* to another at the bar virtually in mid-sentence. She had done the wrong thing, even by working-girl standards. All the other girls knew it, the *mamasan* knew it and, as I finished off what was left of her 'lady drink', I decided to make sure that *she* knew it.

At this point, I must give the other girls at the bar some credit. They noticed my disappointment even though I tried to hide it behind a broad smile and plenty of "no problem for me" responses. It turned out that the pair of interlopers had been to the bar before and my *tee-ruk* had 'been with' her current focus of attention on at least one previous occasion. Each girl came up to me to check that I was OK. In fact, it was more likely that they came over to make sure I was not going to cause any trouble.

The Dutchman's friend could not fail but notice the activity and, putting two and two together, realized what was going on. He slowly moved towards me and asked, non-menacingly, "Is there a problem?" I gently manoeuvred a couple of the ladies between him and me (have I mentioned cowardice as another of my character flaws?) and replied "Not at all, mate. Plenty of beautiful ladies to go around." My wide smile seemed to satisfy him that I was not going to cause a fuss and he retired to his stool.

The next day I didn't go to the bar, not because of what had happened but because I had already made previous arrangements. It coincided nicely with my scheme to teach my indiscreet ex *tee-ruk* a lesson. I knew that the other girls and the *mamasan* would give her a tongue lashing for possibly scaring me away, along with my money, my friends and my friend's money. It worked.

The following evening I returned to some very relieved and happy ladies. I deliberately ignored my relieved but not-so-happy victim. She came out from behind the counter with the purpose of sitting beside me. Her plan was obviously to explain her behaviour, offer a bar girl apology and then we would kiss and make up. I quietly turned my back on her targeted vacant stool beside me and initiated a somewhat one-sided conversation about nuclear physics and the NASA space program with one of the other girls. Petty? Childish? Ok, add them to the list of my character defects. While you are at it, add vengeance. Never giving her the chance to get me alone, in a true slapstick comedy performance I exaggerated the good time I was having with the rest of the staff.

About an hour or so later, the Dutchman's friend turned up alone. He sat at the other end of the bar, ordered a drink and was then ignored by all but the least attractive of the ladies. I was monopolizing all of the other girl's time and having a ball. He must have been seething at the lack of attention coming his way because it eventually got the better of him.

He slowly walked towards me and asked, in heavily accented English, "When do you go home?"

Smiling, I happily replied, "Never. I live here."

"Ugh," he grunted, then turned and walked back to his seat, gulped the remainder of his bottle of Heineken, checked bin and skulked off into the night.

To my knowledge, the Dutchman and his friend never came back to the bar. Whether they returned home or not, I don't know. My ex *tee-ruk* quit work two weeks later and I have not seen her since. I was told she went home, but that is the standard response to any question regarding the whereabouts of a bar girl. She may be working in another bar in Pattaya or Bangkok. In the vengeance department, I would have declared victory except for one truly unfortunate conclusion to this story. Deep down inside of what remained of my shattered bleak heart, I still really liked her.

7

Chicken Anyone?

Ask any expat dropout in Thailand and they will tell you that one of the annoying things about the place is trying to stay here. Legally, that is. Sooner or later, after exhausting the supply of visa extensions, foreigners are faced with what is affectionately known as the 'visa run'. They are obliged to leave the country, come back and start the visa process all over again. The alternative is to risk internment and deportation. If you evade capture, you will be required to cough up 200 *baht* per day of your overstay the next time you attempt to leave the Kingdom. Good for the economy of Thailand but it looks like a "You've been a naughty boy" stamp in your passport.

A short while ago, I was faced with my own visa problem, having run out of extensions and excuses. Mentioning it to a couple of my drinking mates, they explained that they too were on their last days. As luck would have it, our visas all expired within three days of each other. As luck would further have it, one of the guys owned a car. Why don't we do a visa run together? That way we could share the driving and fuel costs. Over quite a few gallons of amber fluid we all agreed it was a great idea and a date was fixed.

On the day of the run we all met at the appointed place at the unearthly hour of 6:00am. I thought God invented Pattaya so that no one would ever have to get up at six in the morning. Nevertheless, it was a fine day and at 6:05 we were on our way to the border crossing at *Poi Pet* in Cambodia, the nearest border point to Pattaya. We were told it was just under four hours drive, very easy to find and the roads were good. All of this turned out to be true.

The problem with driving in Thailand is not the distance, the signposts or the roads. The problem is all the other lunatics driving in Thailand. Just because you consider yourself to be the world's best driver and have not had an accident in forty years, never assume everyone else is. Local driving antics may also lead you to believe that there are no road rules in Thailand. There are rules, it is just that no one follows them and nobody seems to enforce them.

I blame the belief in reincarnation. Moreover, it is the belief that, providing you have led a virtuous life, the next time around you will come back as something better as your reward. Furthermore, every chronic underachiever in Thailand mistakenly believes he has been a decent character in this life and, after shuffling off his current mortal coil, will come back to a bigger house, prettier wife and a better job. Therefore, the belief in reincarnation goes hand in hand with a complete lack of fear of death. This manifests itself the moment a Thai gets behind the wheel of a car, truck or motorbike. Thai road users seem to think they will live forever and nothing could ever happen to them. Statistics prove otherwise and show that road carnage is an effective method of population control. My friends and I do not believe in reincarnation and, as a result, have a real and terrifying fear of death. Even if we did believe in reincarnation, our lives to date have been less than noteworthy so the thought of coming back as a cockroach or dung beetle was equally horrifying.

On the way to *Poi Pet*, my mates shared the driving, two hours on and two hours off. I sat in the back seat having a very religious experience, mostly with my eyes shut. During this forward journey, the other traffic consisted mostly of trucks. Very large and probably overloaded trucks. We were sideswiped, run off the road and had several very exciting games of 'chicken' with oncoming vehicles. Thailand – 4; *fa-lung* – 0. By the time we reached our destination, I had thought of every possible excuse to get out of driving on the way home, including having a sick buffalo needing my care and attention. I had no idea how this popular ploy would relieve me of my share of the driving, but I was a drowning man and I grasped any straws I could find. Unknown to me, my shell-shocked friends in the front seat were also scheming as to how they could make me drive all the way back to Pattaya.

The visa renewal procedure at *Poi Pet* was the easiest part of the trip. It was surprisingly quick and merely involved the usual paperwork, pay, paperwork, pay, paperwork routine. Now I could tell everyone at home that I've been to Cambodia and show my passport to prove it.

With the ink on our visa stamps still wet, we took the opportunity to have a brief look at the large marketplace on the Thai side of the border. The prices were low, the quality was suspect and the touts and beggars were very annoying. After a quick plastic bag of ice-cold soft drink, it was back to the car for the trip home. Imagine my surprise when I was thrown the car keys just before my pals bounced into the back seat. I took the hint and realized my sick buffalo story would never cut it now. Accepting my fate, I made a brief pit stop for fuel and then turned the car for home.

With the two conspirators in the back semiconscious, I decided to take a different route back to Pattaya. The truth is, I got lost. I have been afflicted with navigational problems all my life and to be totally honest, have trouble finding my way to the bathroom in a two-room apartment. Without my friends to prompt me and with my concentration exclusively on the road and vehicles whistling around me, I missed what happened to be a vital turn-off. We were now heading along paths unknown.

About an hour's driving later, I found another turn-off that I hoped would correct my original oversight. At least it was heading in the right direction. I took the chance and, shortly after turning off the main road, sighted what appeared to be a restaurant. It had a large sign out front saying 'Food' in perfect English, so there was a chance we could actually find something to eat there.

The two sleeping beauties in the back seat woke as soon as they heard the engine switch off. I decided not to tell them about my navigational error. Better leave that little surprise for later. With any luck we could be back on the correct road before they realized we had ever been off it and I could save considerable face.

"Feel like something to eat?"

"Sure. I'm starving."

"Me too."

After a brief stretch to get the blood circulation going, we strolled towards the door of the restaurant.

Inside, the two Thai girls in attendance stared at us as we looked around for a suitable table. The restaurant was empty so I assumed their nervous gaze was due to the fact that we were the only customers. I found out later it was something more traumatic than that. Neither of them could understand a word of English so they were mentally drawing straws to see which unlucky one would have to serve us. Once we sat down their nervousness went into overdrive with the realization that the three *fa-lung* were not going to simply look around and leave as they had hoped. We were serious diners. As for me, I must say it was a pleasant change to sit in a real chair instead of those usual little plastic stools. The chairs were still plastic, mind you, but at least they had backs to them.

Our hapless serving wench, the loser of the two, was now frantically searching for something. When she found it, her beaming Thai smile returned and she proudly approached our table with the menu. It was the English version and obviously their only copy going by its state of disrepair. The sixty numbered items on the two-page menu were written in Thai with English subtitles.

Beers were definitely called for. We tried ordering our favourite brands but this was met with blank looks from our hostess. Frank simplified matters by holding up three fingers and saying *"Singha"* in his best Thai voice. This worked, and in no time at all our table was adorned with three lukewarm bottles of Singha accompanied by three tall glasses filled with ice. Now, I don't know about you, but I am

Australian and, in Australia, there are only three beers we do not like –
warm beer, watered-down beer and no beer. Watering down warm beer
with ice is doubly offensive but, at that stage, I would have drunk
anything that was wet. I ignored the eerie rustling sound of my ancestors
turning over in their graves as I carefully poured the beer over the ice.

Thirst taken care of, we returned to the menu. Tony liked the sound
of a beef curry and I quite liked the 'Fash wit vegtabul'. I motioned for
the waitress, held the menu up and pointed enthusiastically to the
numbers corresponding to these two dishes. She nodded in affirmation,
busily scribbled something on a scrap of paper and hastened to the
kitchen. She obviously had a short-term memory problem. Frank had
still not decided what he wanted to eat but that was nothing unusual.

Moments later the waitress returned with a concerned look on her
face. "No hab", she whispered.
"You don't have? Which one don't you have?" was my response.
Puzzled look. I pointed to my choice on the menu. "This one?" She
shook her head. "What about this one?" Pointing to Tony's selection
also resulted in a shake of the head. Ok guys, back to the drawing
board. Tony and I each made another selection and Frank too had finally
made up his mind. Beef and noodles, fish barbecue and pork with rice.
Our choices communicated to the waitress with some more finger
pointing. A smile, a nod, some busy scribbling and off she went again.
Frank again held up three fingers and yelled "*Singha*" as she disappeared
through the doorway.

She returned to our table with that now all-too-familiar look on her
face. "No hab."
I pointed to the menu. "This one?" She shook her head.
"What about this one?" More head shaking.
"And this one?"
Three strikes you're out. By this stage Tony was getting a little impatient,
not to mention hungry.
"To save time, why don't you tell us which ones you do have?"
The girl, totally confused, turned and walked back to the kitchen, leaving
us to mull over our bad luck in being able to pick the only five items on

"... it may have been a third rate fighter,
but it sure made a first rate second course!"

the menu that were unavailable. We did not even get our beer. Suddenly a Thai man emerged from the kitchen and headed for our table.

"Shit, we're in trouble now," whispered Frank.

As it turned out, Frank need not have been worried. The man smiled as he reached the table.

"Solly sir. We no hab what you order."
Tony was the first to respond. "Can you tell us what you do have? We're very hungry."

"Chicken. Hab chicken."

"You don't have any pork, beef or fish?"

"No. Hab chicken", he happily replied. "Yesterday very big fighting. Big cock fighting. Many chicken die."

Our laughter surprised him somewhat but he joined in anyway. The relief at finally discovering why we were having trouble ordering was immeasurable.

"Right then. We'll have the chicken curry, the barbecue chicken and the fried chicken." Tony did not even bother with the menu.

"No poblem", smiled the chef as he turned and headed back towards the kitchen. Our three beers then arrived via a very relieved and beaming waitress.

The meal of chicken done every which way but loose was excellent, made even more so by the rapid exchange of morbid chicken jokes between the three of us. There was general agreement that next time we should plan our trip so we could go to the cockfighting and see what sort of lacklustre performance our intended meal put up. Tony wanted to know whether the victorious cock looked up into the cheering crowd in search of 'thumbs down' signals before delivering the coup de grace. The finale was when Frank, patting his stomach, exclaimed that "it may have been a third rate fighter, but it sure made a first rate second course!"

8

Where You Come From?

I t all began because I was getting bored with being asked, "Where you come from?" by every bar girl each time I planted my substantial derriere on a bar stool. This is one of the first two questions Thai girls ask any new foreigner who sits at their bar. Geography was never one of their strong points, so wherever you come from, they probably have no idea where it is. It got to the point where I would change my nationality alphabetically to add a bit of variety. I was from Australia, then Bulgaria, then Canada, Dubai, England, France, Germany and so on. It has been fun up until now, but the problem is that I am up to 'x' and have been racking my brain trying to think of a country starting with 'x'. Is 'Xanadu' a country?

Game-playing aside, I became interested in reversing the roles and asking each bar girl, "Where do you come from?" To date, the feedback from the girls begs the question; "Would the last female between the ages of eighteen and thirty to leave *Korat*, please turn off the lights?"

From my research, I estimate that 70% of the working girls of Pattaya come from the northeastern region of Thailand, a region known as *Isaan*. Bordering Laos to the north and east and Cambodia to the south, it is Thailand's poorest and most populous region, being home to just over one-third of Thailand's population. In the southwestern corner of *Isaan* is *Korat* (pronounced *Ko-lart*), but the chances are you will not find it marked on any map. It is the local name for the province of *Nakon Ratchisima* which, in area, is Thailand's largest province. Outside of Bangkok, it is also Thailand's most populous province.

Just because you came to Pattaya for a month's holiday and did not meet one girl who comes from *Korat* does not make my statement about their predominance false. Given more time, I'm sure you would discoveras I did, that the percentage of bar girls who said they come from *Korat* would increase sufficiently enough to make them the largest single demographic group.

Still in *Isaan* but heading east of *Nakon Ratchisima*, we have *Buri Ram, Surin, Sri Sa Ket* and *Ubon Ratchathani*. To the north and northeast , you will hear names like *Roi Et, Khon Kaen, Udon Thani* and *Nong Khai*, which is right on the Lao border. Almost all *Isaan* girls can speak Lao as well as Thai and are usually easy to pick out from a crowd because they will be the ones buying or chewing on insects. As a general rule, girls from other regions don't eat bugs.

Twenty percent of the bar girl population come from the eastern region, from places like *Prachin Buri, Sa Kaeo, Chonburi, Chantaburi* and *Rayong*. The remaining ten percent come from the near-north and northwest of Bangkok – places like *Sara Buri, Lopburi, Nakon Sawan, Phet Chabun* and *Kam Phaeng Phet*. Few come from further north since they have a long distance to travel in order to get to Pattaya. They could just as easily go to Bangkok or *Chiang Mai*, the second largest city in Thailand, as travel to Pattaya. Very few come from the southern parts of Thailand or from Bangkok and I have yet to meet a girl working in a bar who was actually born and raised in Pattaya.

There are many factors which affect the population mix of bar girls in Pattaya, the most significant being the economy of the regions they come from. It should come as no surprise that the northeast area of Thailand is the poorest in the country and offers the least job opportunities. But the girls from *Isaan* have a choice. Why not work in Bangkok, in areas like Patpong, Nana or *Soi* Cowboy? Some do, but Bangkok is a huge city and very intimidating for a rural Thai girl.

Pattaya, on the other hand, is like a large country town. Although it has the necessary components - big name hotels, bars, tourists - to define it as a cosmopolitan centre, so far it has retained its rural beginnings in a way that does not frighten off a simple country girl. Many people from *Isaan* are already living and working in Pattaya so the new arrival does not feel so isolated.

Bangkok also has a reputation for being a 'dangerous' place. It is probably no more dangerous than any other city its size in the world, but to the rural communities who get most of their information from watching television news broadcasts, the nightly summary of crime and mayhem in the capital must really scare them.

Looking at a map of Thailand, it is easy to see why the girls from the southeast would come here. It is the first major population centre on the road to Bangkok and there are many buses going direct to Pattaya. Those from the north must pass through Bangkok to get here but again, the same factors come into play as for the girls from *Isaan* as to why some prefer to work in Pattaya.

Why don't many girls from Bangkok come to work in Pattaya? Because these girls are usually more sophisticated and being brought up in the big city, Pattaya is too provincial for them. There are also plenty of bars in Bangkok to choose from in areas away from view of their family and friends.

What about local girls, those born and bred in Pattaya? Firstly, since Pattaya was only a small fishing village thirty years ago, there are not many 'local' girls to speak of. Secondly, those who were born here are from a different socioeconomic class to the bar girls. Their parents have had access to more money, they have had better opportunities and have usually reached a higher level of education. The family may operate a business in which case, they already have a ready-made job. Thirdly, they are not likely to work as bar girls in their home town with their parents, relatives and friends nearby. There is still a social stigma attached to working as a bar girl and she would never be allowed to cause any loss of face to her family.

So there we have the demographics of the Pattaya bar scene. The blend of cultures, values and traditions makes for a fascinating study but, in the final synopsis, we can not escape the reality of what Pattaya is all about - the daughters of Thailand's rural community coming together for the common good - money.

9

Rags to Riches

This is not one of those typical 'poor boy makes good' vomituous tales of how hard work and fortuitous insight enabled a rat-eating pauper to crawl his way out of the mire. Neither is it a self-indulgent narrative of a fellow suffering from abject poverty and living in squalor who managed, through strong moral fibre and intestinal fortitude, to turn around his financial woes and ended up owning a small country. This story is different because I am still at the abject poverty and living in squalor stage, having not yet made it up one rung of the financial ladder. There was a temptation to write this story in the third person in an attempt to hide the fact that it was autobiographical, but it would fool no one. The moment any of my acquaintances read the tale of woe, they would easily recognize the hapless *fa-lung*. I have lost so much face already that it is difficult to see my reflection in the bathroom mirror.

Last week, I decided to sell my television set. This was particularly traumatic and, before pulling the plug for the last time, I spent some time simply staring over at the very forlorn set and wondering what that corner of the room would look like without its majestic presence. If I had not already sold my camera, I would have taken a photo to remember it by. Television had become my last bastion of free entertainment and I so enjoyed watching the news bulletins that filled the screen daily with reports of wars, floods, famine and riots. In my cocoon of self-pity, those vivid images would always cheer me up because it was nice to know that there were, in fact, people worse off than me. But all good things must come to an end and it was with great sadness and lying tongue that I took my beautiful TV set back to the shop where it was purchased, explaining that I was moving to a bigger apartment that already had a TV. I may not have any self-respect but I do still have my pride. Anyone want to buy some pride?

As many foreign males staying in Thailand will confirm, the best quality of a live-in Thai girlfriend is the support and comfort they can provide their partner when desperate times call for desperate measures. My delicate little Thai flower, once she returned home from her daily gossiping session, took the news quite well. An hour of screaming interfused with periods of ranting and raving in what could only be described as extremely unladylike Thai. Once she settled down, there was silence. A long period of silence. Next came a very long period of silence, followed by a full day of deafening silence. Neither inducement nor threat would make her budge from the sanctuary of the bed, where she would prop herself up against the pillows in pathetic mimicry of a person watching television.

To be truthful, the peace and quiet was just starting to become pleasant when it stopped as suddenly as it started. First came the hint of a smile, then eye contact and a gaze of recognition followed by those poetic words that every *fa-lung* finds so endearing.
"*Tee-ruk?*"
I was off the hook, or so it seemed.
"I have idea."

Of all the words I wanted to hear next, these were not them. The Marquis de Sade was a pussy cat compared to the pain and suffering that could be inflicted by a Thai girl with an 'idea'. My heart sank in Titanic proportions with the realization that all the while she had been giving me the cold shoulder, she had been quietly scheming.
"Darling, you know I don't like you thinking. You could hurt something, probably me."
That went straight over her head, thankfully.

"I make *ka-nom Thai* [sweet Thai desserts]. Sell in market. Make money every day."
This from a woman who once told me that her own mother banned her from the family kitchen because she could not boil water. It was worse than I thought.

"Have book", she proudly announced, handing me a hard-covered Thai recipe book. It was full of pretty pictures and probably some complicated Thai instructions to go with them.
"Are you sure you can make these?"
It was difficult not to sound too condescending.
"Yes. I have one thousand *baht*. I buy everything tomorrow."

More of which I did not want to hear. I knew where she kept her one thousand *baht* and I was saving this as my emergency slush fund should I ever be asked to leave at short notice. It would pay for a bus to *Don Muang*, the airport departure tax and a couple of farewell beers. However, she seemed excited about her project and no longer wanted to cut my heart out with a spoon. Reluctant acquiescence seemed the only option. There was a minuscule chance that her business enterprise could work. I don't believe I said that.

The following evening, I returned from my day out scavenging food to discover that my postage stamp sized kitchen had been struck by a psychedelic atom bomb. The array of colours plastered to the walls, table and floor resembled a 1970's style apartment occupied by someone called 'Rainbow'. There is no God, because if there were, he would have sent a bolt of lightning to fry me to a crisp and thus end my suffering there and then. But no, this was to be my punishment for selling the television.

Ignoring the disarray for the time being, I noticed a pristine red plastic stool in the centre of the room. A cane basket filled with goodies, hygienically packaged in non-Greenpeace approved cellophane and polystyrene, adorned the floor beside the stool. Giving credit where credit is due, the finished products did look appealing. Grinning like a Cheshire cat, the cook certainly looked pleased with herself.

"How much for these?" I inquired of my smiling little genius.
"Twenty *baht.*"
A quick count revealed ten neatly packaged morsels of brightly-coloured desserts.
"That means you sell all and get 200 *baht*?"
"No. Twenty *baht.* Sell only one, two *baht.*"
"How do you get to the market?"
"Motorcycle."

Total disbelief descended like a veil and mercifully rendered me speechless. The motorcycle ride to the market would cost her twenty *baht*, then she would be required to pay a token rent for her square metre of space. She would need another twenty *baht* for the motorcycle ride home, since she could not be expected to walk after such an enterprising and tiring day out. Not forgetting, of course, her initial outlay for the ingredients.

Without a word, I cleaned up the mess that once was my kitchen, washing and drying each piece of offensive cookware and stacking them neatly on top of the wardrobe, safely out of reach of female hands. It was best to remove the knives and other sharp objects first. They were placed safely out of the reach of my hands, because the prospect of murder, suicide or both became very real to me. She sat and watched in silence, but I could tell that my message was understood.

For several days the dinner menu consisted of a load of Thai desserts. The good news was that the love of my life agreed to never ever do any more thinking. She must leave that to the professionals, those with more than one brain cell. The desserts have finally run out and if anyone out there would like a good rat recipe, I have many which, for the price of a drumstick, I will gladly share with you.

52

10

The Phone Call

❝What the bloody hell are you doing in Thailand?" The voice down
the telephone line sounded more shocked than inquisitive. Still, it
was a fair question and it got me thinking. Leaving Thailand's
obvious attractions aside, I wondered why I love the place so much and
never want to leave.

I could confess to my friend that, when I look back at forty years
spent in Australia, I cannot remember ever really feeling that I was
home. On reflection, my life there was spent on a continual search for
that special place where I felt I belonged. Every stage of my life,
everywhere I lived, every house I owned and every job I held was a
temporary measure, a fill-in, a stopgap until all the pieces of the jigsaw
puzzle fell into place. So why Thailand? Why did everything have to
synchronize here? What is it about Thailand that made me want to stay
here?

I could tell him that I love the weather. Thailand is hot and sometimes
hot and wet, but I like the 'hot' and can tolerate 'wet'. This is probably
due to my English ancestry. Consider, if you will, the older maps of the
world. Most of the red bits lie between the Tropic of Cancer and the
Tropic of Capricorn. This is not by accident. I believe early English
explorers were neither overly intrepid nor were they exceptionally brave,
they were just sick of being cold all the time. Every Englishman with

get-up-and-go, got up and went. The moment he got the chance, he turned his ship towards the equator and took pot luck. I have merely done the same thing except I started from a different hemisphere.

I could talk about the wonderful food. As a child I can remember Chinese takeaway nights as a highlight of the week. It wasn't until my first trip to Hong Kong in 1980 that I discovered that the Chinese takeaway was not really Chinese at all. They were Western dishes with Chinese sounding names made for Western palates and were unheard of in true Chinese cuisine. I found the true Asian fare to be even more exciting and varied than the modified version I was served in Australia.

I also like my food hot. The Thai restaurants in Australia toned down the spices, so I tried Indian cooking. It was not until I tasted Thai food here in Thailand that I found the variety and mix of spices and flavours that are a true delight. I still enjoy Indian curries but Thai dishes don't have the religious restrictions that limit many Indian menus.

I could say I enjoy being in a mostly Buddhist country. The truth is I am a devout atheist who has no interest in organized religion whatsoever. I believe in live-and-let-live and, as long as someone doesn't try and ram their own beliefs down my throat, I don't care if they are Maypole-dancing tree-worshipping Druids. Imagine my delight in learning that Buddhism is not really a religion but a way of life. It is a gentle way of life and no Buddhist has ever come knocking on my door and tried to convert me or worse, tried to save my soul. I am also a devout coward, a card-carrying member of Invertebrates Anonymous. It is interesting to note that no crusade or war has ever been waged in the name of Buddha, and Buddhists have been around for five hundred years longer than Christians.

I could speak about the Thai people and their culture, from their traditions to their liking for ceremony. I love their respect for their elders (a group to which I now unhappily belong) and their removal of shoes before entering a house. I love the *wai*-ing and the festive occasions such as *Loi Grathong* and *Songkran*, although *Songkran* is actually wearing a bit thin after four consecutive years of it.

54

I could tell him that, although the cost of living in Pattaya may be high by Thai standards, it is affordable by Western standards. I only need to live simply and comfortably, and can do so at bargain prices. Thailand is inexpensive for foreigners as long as they stay out of the bars, foreign restaurants and obvious tourist traps. Thai food from exclusively Thai restaurants is cheap and filling. Western restaurants and Thai restaurants selling Western food are more expensive because they cater to foreigners who are willing to pay more for a meal. Limiting my patronage of bars is difficult but necessary in order to prevent a severe drain on finances.

I could explain the bleeding obvious. I can hear the feminists shrieking but it has been my experience that a single heterosexual male in Australia who is overweight and over forty is on the scrap heap as far as attracting the opposite sex goes. The only women he may tempt are overbearing, overweight and over sixty. So what is he to do? Be content with a life of celibacy or worse, grab-a-granny nights? Thailand offers hope because neither age nor body mass is a disadvantage for a man. If a sixty-year-old man has a belly that looks like he is about to give birth to twins, it doesn't seem to matter to Thais. It shows he can afford to eat well.

Sure, it all comes down to money, but so what. If a fat man in his sixties finds happiness with the care and affection, whether genuine or not, of an attractive twenty-five year old girl, good luck to him. And if that same lady achieves her goal of being cared for and provided for by him, good luck to her also. As long as the man knows the score and is sensible, it is a win-win situation. She receives financial security for herself and her family and he receives the kind of attention he could only dream about back home.

I could spell out that, to me, Thailand is just one big twenty-four hour convenience store. In Pattaya, I can usually get anything I want any time I want it without having to travel great distances to do so. If I wake up at three o'clock in the morning thirsty, hungry, with a headache or in need of company, everything I need is within five minutes walk. More often than not, the supermarket comes to me. Every day, vendors selling food, goods and chattels parade past my door. If they don't have it, my local grocery store delivers. All it takes is a phone call.

In Australia, many places close by eleven o'clock, so whenever I was in desperate need of a pack of cigarettes at three in the morning, it usually involved a long drive to an all-night supermarket or service station. If I had one or two beers under my belt, it meant going without rather than risk apprehension by the constabulary. Those night-stalkers delighted in stopping vehicles that dared to sneak along deserted streets at a time when respectable people were asleep.

I could report that traveling around Pattaya, for someone without his own means of transport, is also very easy. The much-maligned *baht* bus is an efficient and cheap means of getting around the city. On most occasions I can travel from one side of Pattaya to the other in less than twenty minutes. Whenever more speed is called for, there are motorcycle taxis. I admit these are my least favoured means of transport and I use them sparingly, but they are quick. No more telephoning for a taxi and waiting thirty minutes for it to arrive if, in fact, it ever arrived at all. No more walking a kilometre to the bus stop or train station. My transport now comes right to my front door and most of the time, stops where I want it to stop.

How can you explain this to someone who has never been outside his own country? How can you describe in a few words, at international call rates, that you have found what you've been looking for all of your life? Finally, my silence brought about the logical follow-up to his opening question.
"When are you coming home?"
Without hesitation, the words fell from my lips.
"I *am* home."

11

Relatively Speaking

It was my second morning in *Kam Phaeng Phet*. The love of my life, *Nong*, her Mama, Papa, her five year old son and two other people whose relationship remains a mystery, were sitting on the floor slowly picking at the bountiful food placed before them.

The dust from the bus trip from Pattaya had finally vacated the pores in my skin thanks to the three brisk open-air showers I had taken since arrival, ladling the freezing cold well water over my shivering torso. Modesty aside, outdoor showers take a lot of getting used to. When you have lathered up your hair and head then cannot find the ladle, it is particularly unpleasant. I must have looked like a giant ice-cream cone stumbling around their back yard.

My heart palpitations had also subsided. Here's a tip for anyone planning a trip to beautiful *Kam Phaeng Phet* by bus. Never arrive at 1:00am. The bus terminal is not quite in the centre of town and public transport is nonexistent at that time. The only means of transportation is motorcycle. *Nong's* home is outside of town anyway, so she did some negotiating with a couple of likely lads who seemed not too pleased at being awakened from their Thai-nap. This, of course, was reflected in their fee. Haggling completed, *Nong* moved towards the better-looking of the two bikes while, fresh from his Mekong-induced coma, my personal torturer signalled for me to mount his rather suspect bike.

For you to fully appreciate the gravity of the situation, I should point out that I had ridden a motorcycle only twice before in my life. I hate motorcycles. My philosophy is why should I settle for something with two wheels when there are plenty around with four. And sides. And a roof. And seat-belts. This night I had no choice. There was an added bonus. *Nong* had graciously allowed me to carry the suitcase. I usually travel light – very light. Back in Pattaya she decided that my small carry bag was insufficient to contain her wardrobe of absolute necessities. She convinced (ordered) me to bring my suitcase. The case itself weighs 3kg. My personal items weigh about 2kg so, packed with *Nong's* essentials, the whole thing weighed close to 30kg. At the time, I weighed 90kg and my non-Thai-smiling driver appeared to be no more than 50kg. I don't know how much the bike weighed, but I was certain that it was not enough to bear the burden.

Once on the back of the bike, there was no way to position the suitcase in order for it to balance. The only way to carry it was to hold it in one hand out from the side of the bike, away from any moving bits. Thus we set off, *Nong* sitting cool and comfortable on the leading machine with enough room to dance the tango if she so desired, and me, a lump of jelly performing a balancing act that Barnham and Bailey would have been proud of.

This was still not enough. In Thailand, outside of Bangkok, Pattaya and other tourist areas, there is nobody about at one o'clock in the morning. The streets are deserted - no traffic, no police. What happens when you get two young Thai males, partially sober, on motorcycles with empty streets ahead of them? You guessed it. They decided to test out their respective machines, clear all the day's dust from the carburettors and, once and for all, determine which bike was the best, i.e. fastest. There are no words in the English language which fully describe my feelings as we sped, two abreast, through the narrow, dark streets. 'Fear' and 'horror' do not even come close. It was a long twenty minutes.

Upon arrival at *Nong's* home, they called for an oxy-torch to break the weld my knees had formed with the sides of the bike. I dismounted

58

and literally kissed the ground – Pope style. None of the family could speak English, but it did not matter because the only sounds emanating from my mouth were sort of blubbering, gurgling noises.

Back at the dining mat, the conversation continued. With occasional glances at me, I guessed they were planning some activity for the day. Eventually, *Nong* explained that we would go to visit her Grandfather. He lived about an hour's drive away and was *mai sa-bai* because his doctor had told him to stop drinking. I understood his unhappiness. She further explained that we would not stay overnight because Grandfather's home was 'primitive'. She implied that it was my comfort she was thinking of, but having known her for some time, I was in no doubt it was actually her pampered little derrière she was considering.

Nong's father owned a car, a well-kept, white, four-door sedan. On an earlier occasion she tried to explain to me what he did for a living and after a prolonged game of charades, I concluded he was either a fireman, water-delivery man, drove an ambulance or he worked for the city council. No matter, his car at least had four wheels.

Later that morning, we all piled into what should have been a comfortable car. Papa, of course, was the driver. *Nong* sat in the middle of the front seat while I held the window, or suicide seat. Mama, *Nong's* son, another small child and the two mysterious people filled the back seat. The trunk was loaded with supplies (food) for Grandfather.

The first stop was for fuel. I offered to pay but it was a totally unnecessary gesture, since I was fully expected to pay in any case. As the drive continued, I noticed that the roads were getting narrower and the people scarce. An hour later we were on a dirt track that I would not have attempted even in a four-wheel-drive vehicle. No problem. No one seemed concerned. They were not even concerned at the rain clouds developing off in the distance. I spent some time imagining what the road would be like coming back - in the dark and the rain.

We had progressed further along the track when Papa suddenly stopped the car in the middle of nowhere. For a fleeting second I thought that this was the end of me - they were going to kill me for the money they thought I had and bury my body in a shallow grave never to be found. Luckily, this turned out not to be the case. I asked *Nong* what the problem was. She said they thought they saw Grandfather. Papa put the car in reverse and, with the skill of a tank driver traversing through a minefield, reversed the vehicle back about a hundred metres to a shanty beside the road. It was so small that I hadn't noticed what turned out to be a shop which sold provisions to the local community.

Out front, sitting on a small bamboo chair at a small bamboo table, was an old barefoot gentleman sitting alone. He had the physique of a man half his age. The only thing that gave away his age was his leathery skin. There are some crocodile handbags in the world that will wear away before his hide does. On the table in front of him was a large half-full (or half-empty, depending on your point of view) bottle of *Singha* and a full glass. Underneath the table were three large empty bottles of the same brew.

Papa stopped the car opposite his table and pleasantries were exchanged.
"I thought you told me that Grandfather was *mai sa-bai* because his doctor told him he could not drink?" I asked an excited *Nong*. She shrugged her shoulders.
"*Mai roo.*"
Good on him, I thought. Who listens to doctors anyway? What do they know?

A few minutes later and my hand was again introduced to my pocket. I purchased six large bottles of *Singha* plus paid for the ones the old guy had already consumed. Don't mention it. Off we went again. With no more room in the car, Grandfather opted to take the short-cut home, through the bush.

We soon arrived at our destination. Actually, we arrived at a clearing in the forest. There seemed to be a large pile of bamboo accompanied by two smaller piles nearby. After fording a small stream (my thoughts returned to those threatening rain clouds), Papa parked the car in a shaded area. Grandfather was already there to meet us. It seems he was not only old, stubborn and a drunk, but a superb cross-country sprinter as well. He descended from inside the largest stack of bamboo. That was his house. One of the smaller stacks was a type of visitors' cottage or guest room. The other one? Well, maybe it was just a pile of spare bamboo for repairs, renovations and extensions.

For the next hour I was left basically to myself. Our visit must have been announced over the short wave or tom–toms because people kept appearing out of the forest to see the stupid *fa-lung* that *Nong* had captured. The trunk of the car was emptied of booty and the women all seemed to want to prepare the food, or at least, comment on its quality. Later, I was offered a not-too-cold beer and sat around with the menfolk as we swapped jokes, complained about women, caught up on all the sporting news and generally had a good time. At least I think that's what we were doing. None of them could speak English and their pronunciation of Thai was not exactly out of the textbook. Anyway, that is what we would have done back home, so I assumed that men are the same the world over.

The afternoon progressed and the women prepared a sumptuous meal before the candles were lit. Grandfather had no electricity, no telephone, no water and, as I was soon to find out, no toilet. The stream nearby served as his drinking water supply, his bath/shower, his washing machine and his flush toilet. Isn't Mother Nature wonderful?

As darkness fell, out came the meal and the mosquitoes. Not the same garden variety that plague the rest of the world, these were the size of grasshoppers. These suckers had a voracious appetite. Just four of them could drain an elephant. It was then that I realized that *Nong* and her extended family were all sitting down the other end of the room. I was on my Pat Malone. While the mosquitoes were satisfying their hunger with the newly-acquired taste for *fa-lung* royal blue blood, my hosts were sitting as far away as possible, in relative comfort. It appeared that they had either forgotten about me or were using me to attract the insects away from themselves. I soon put a stop to that and joined the rest of the group.

The meal was typical Thai and typically delicious. *Nong* had already explained to them that I could eat hot food without any problem. One dish in particular I found very tasty. It was slices of meat doused in chili, but it had an unusual taste and texture. In the three candlepower half-light, I could not tell if it was white or dark meat.

"Not *neu-a*," *Nong* explained.

I knew the Thai words for chicken, pork and fish, so I came to the conclusion, correctly, that '*neu-a*' meant 'beef'. Well, if it was not beef, what the hell was it? I recalled that, in many parts of Asia, they eat dog meat. This was not a happy thought after having devoured half a bowl of the stuff. *Nong* said something in Thai then, realizing that I did not understand, went into charade mode. With three fingers from each hand extended, she placed a hand on each side of her head, above her ears. It did not take Einstein to work out that she was imitating antlers and thus, a deer.

"Deer? You mean deer?" I exclaimed with relief.

"Yes," she replied. "Grandfather shoot in park."

Confusion over, I settled down to a delicious venison meal washed down with ample beer. As soon as the meal was over, we packed up and headed home.

The following day, back in *Kam Phaeng Phet*, I learned that, adjoining Grandfather's property, was a National Park - a flora and fauna reserve full of protected plants, birds and (surprise, surprise!) deer. It seemed that, as well as being a true character, a heavy drinker and an excellent runner, ol' Granddad was also a poacher.

12

The Butterfly Myth

In our own countries we would call him a philanderer or adulterer, but the Thais have a much more colourful name for the wandering male of our species – a Butterfly. Why does a man 'butterfly' in Pattaya? This is similar to asking, "why does a male dog lick his balls?" Because he can! Pattaya is a flowering garden, a true butterfly Nirvana, with an abundance of beautiful temptations.

Being the voracious researcher that I am, some time ago I decided to investigate these most accursed of Pattaya's creatures. I thought it would make interesting reading to do some case studies for male readers to admire and any female readers to disdain. It is now my sad duty to report that, after studying the behavioural patterns and habits of the Pattaya Butterfly, including several failed attempts at emulating his lifestyle, I have drawn the conclusion that he does not exist. At least, not in the pure form. So it is time to explode the 'Butterfly' myth and file it away in the archives of Pattaya folklore, fiction section.

Comedian Woody Allen once quipped, "sex without love is a meaningless experience but, as meaningless experiences go, it's pretty damned good!" Basically, the idea of noncommittal sex with multiple partners is not a new one. It has been around since man first ventured out of his cave and clobbered the first female (not necessarily human) that he happened across. Once satisfied, he would return to his cave, fall asleep and wait until his primal urges rose again. To many of us, they were the good old days.

In the 21st Century, the caveman scenario is played out daily in the streets of Pattaya. The modern day caveman, however, ventures out of his hotel and uses his wallet, not a club, to score the first female his loins desire. Once satisfied, he can bide his time until he again feels the need. This is where the similarity ends and fortunately, or unfortunately, the only genuine 'Butterfly', the original caveman, followed the dinosaur into oblivion.

My first case study involved a friend, actually an acquaintance, who I considered to be a true Butterfly. His exploits in *Soi* 6 were legendary. At the beginning of his vacation, two short-times a day were his minimum achievement and his hotel room was 'out of bounds'. He once explained to me what the definition of 'eternity' was: "Eternity is that interval of time between when I cum and she goes." Romantic fool!

I asked him for some advice on how to be a Butterfly. His answer was simple - tell the truth. Tell each new girl you meet that you are a Butterfly or helicopter and that you have many girlfriends. They will appreciate the fact that you have been honest and will know in advance that any relationship with you will be strictly business and strictly short-term. Any girl looking for a more substantial relationship will be put off but truthfully, a Butterfly didn't want someone like that anyway. On the other hand, some girls may even take the declaration as a challenge and give extra special attention in an attempt to cure you of your philandering ways.

He was a hero and, when he returned home, his story was retold in bars the length and breadth of Pattaya. His bravado and self-assuredness led me to believe that no little darling could ever pierce his armoured hide. That was until I learned that he left some money with another friend to be given to one of his conquests, along with his e-mail address. He was a fraud. As we all know, the slightest fissure can bring down a jetliner and one bar girl had reached through his armour, captured his

64

heart and held it for ransom. A true Butterfly would never have let this happen and I lost many illusions.

Case number two, another friend, was a confirmed bachelor at home and an active hedonist in Pattaya. His day consisted of one short-time every afternoon or early evening followed by a drinking session with his mates. I asked him what the secret was to being a Butterfly. He answered that he only ever went short time and never used his hotel room. This was the key to being a Butterfly. He argued that if a man takes a girl back to his hotel for an overnighter, by showing her where he is staying, he has given away a valuable advantage.

He hunted in the short-time bars, late afternoon being the best time. This ensured that the whereabouts of his hotel room or cave remained a secret. It also meant that any repeat performance with the girl was entirely up to him. She could not track him down or telephone his hotel room to initiate a subsequent date. Because it is easier to get a girl in Pattaya than it is to get rid of one, he sometimes even changed hotels at some point of his stay to add a bit of variety and reduce the chances of being discovered by an ex-conquest.

Alas, it transpired that, in a moment of weakness, he forgot his rule and allowed a girl back to his room. She sneaked under his guard and his carefully laid strategy and he went back for seconds. Then thirds. The last time he went to see her she was not at her usual bar. After he returned home, I received an e-mail from him asking if I could find out where she was working. He wanted to see her again when he came back to Pattaya. Another one bites the dust.

My final case study was not a 'Butterfly' in the strictest sense, but close enough to warrant mentioning. His strategy was not the same as the previous two. He did not like short-time, preferring to take the girl back to his hotel overnight. He enjoyed the companionship and intimacy as well as the sex.

He had what he called his 'harem' of six girls he would visit on a weekly basis. (Yes, he took one night off for rest and recovery.) Each girl knew about the others and knew which was her night. If she was busy with another *fa-lung* on her rostered night, he would simply freelance and find a substitute. Good plan and it worked well for a long time. That was until he started to 'double-up' with one of his harem. She took over two nights per week. Pretty soon it was three and now, she is his permanent houseguest.

"What can I do?" he confessed, "She is terrific. I've never met anyone like her." Yet another pair of wings clipped.

An obvious conclusion to draw from these three examples is that in Pattaya, the male Butterfly, like his namesake in nature, has a very short life span. Holiday-makers seemed to have the best chances of survival. My research showed that the longer a man stayed here, the more chance he had of falling by the wayside. One week or a month usually did not allow enough time to really get attached to one lady and surrender the Butterfly tag.

Why is this so? Surely this is the lifestyle that most men have dreamed about since they first noticed a curly hair sprout in their nether regions. True, but it is said that for each of us there is a perfect mate out there just waiting to be found. One major hazard of being a Butterfly is that he will eventually find her. Mathematically he can't miss. Sooner or later one lady will have all the qualities that he subconsciously desires and he will not want to let her go.

I decided to test this theory by asking the ones who should know the answer and, if I caught them sober, may even understand the question - the expats.

Ninety percent of those I spoke with already had a live-in Thai partner. Even though this disqualified them from being true Butterflies, with so few others to interrogate, I needed to at least check their opinions. What was it like for the long-term visitors and the expats who have made Pattaya their home?

The consensus was that yes, the men with wives or steady girlfriends butterfly a little, or would like to. Some butterfly a lot, or would like to. Pattaya provided the perfect environment for a man to sow a wild oat or two but they did not butterfly as often as one would expect. There are three reasons why.

Firstly, being a Butterfly is not as glamorous as it sounds. I know it is stating the obvious, but there has to be a greater risk of STD infection by having sex with multiple partners who are also having sex with multiple partners. Hopefully all would-be Butterflies are sensible enough to use condoms but, with or without protection, the risk of disease must be higher.

Secondly, Pattaya is such a small place that they would eventually get caught by their partner. One guy told me that he slipped out of the house late one afternoon to do a bit of reconnaissance, ending up far away from his home in a *soi* he rarely visited at a bar he had never been to before. He had not even finished his first drink when his mobile phone rang. It was his 'wife' telling him not to stay out too long. He was about to tell her some lie about where he was and what he was doing when she told him the name of the bar he was sitting in. Astounded, he asked her how she knew. She casually replied, "How many eyes has a pineapple?" Last I heard he went to Bangkok to check out the costume shops for a false beard and moustache.

Some attached men I met were smart enough to ask their wife's permission before sowing an oat. At first, to Westerners, this may seem to be an idiotic notion, but in Thailand as in much of Asia, wives are very practical about these matters. They know and understand the nature of man and realize they would never be able to stop him from straying if he put his mind to it. They also understand his occasional need for sex for sex's sake. One lady told me she realized that a man "could not eat chicken every day." As a result, many Thai wives or girlfriends will give permission for their man to have sex with another woman, but they will set the ground rules.

It must not be with anyone she knows and he should go as far away as possible. It must be short-time only, never with the same girl more than once and he must use a condom every time. This way, the wife will not lose face and the chances of him forming a lasting relationship with the girl and her possibly becoming his *mia noi* are reduced. Hopefully, he will not contract an STD to pass on to his spouse.

The last reason has to do with the male psyche. I don't fully understand this but it has something to do with the thrill of the chase. Having a casual sexual relationship here is just too easy. There is no challenge. The male's ego, desperate as it is to be fed, realizes it was not his attractiveness nor his physical abilities that enticed the new lady into bed, but the money he paid her afterwards. Therefore his sexual appetite may be fed but his ego is still hungry for confirmation that he has not lost his appeal to the fairer sex.

The results of my research were disappointing. There must be a lot of men stalking the *sois* of Pattaya who think they are Butterflies but, are they really? Can any male keep sex as purely a business deal? The men did stray from time to time but, considering the availability of obliging ladies in this town, the males disproved the populist theories and feminist charges and displayed a remarkably monogamous character.

13

Doggy Bag

It was his first trip to Thailand so, in true friend style, I went to Bangkok airport to meet him and escort him to Pattaya. Actually, he was a seasoned traveler already but only throughout Europe and the US. Somehow, Asia had always escaped his travel plans and I had a problem convincing him to come over at all. I think he only gave in to shut me up because I never stopped talking about how wonderful Thailand and Pattaya were. In retrospect, this was not one of my brightest ideas because I was now under intense pressure to ensure his holiday was every bit as good as I had promised. What if he got sick? What if he got mugged or hit by a motorcycle? What if he had a terrible time? All of these thoughts kept running through my head as I boarded the bus for the airport. The only solution seemed to be to volunteer myself as his official food-taster, throw myself between any menacing vehicle and his tender flesh and to pray to any God who was listening to please hold off on the rain for a week or so.

A few weeks before he was due to leave, I e-mailed him several pages of instructions on what to do once he exits the customs area at *Don Muang*. Like a doting mother concerned about her son's first day at school, my orders were specific.

"Once you leave customs, turn left and walk towards the barricaded section where I should be waiting. Don't listen to anyone offering taxis, hotels or free rides. Don't leave that area of the terminal building."

Expats living in Asia will tell you never to have only one plan. You must also have an alternate plan, Plan B, to cover the all-too-often occasions that Plan A fails. In many cases it is advisable to have Plan's C and D.

"If I am not there, wait for me for two hours. After two hours, go to the Thai Limousine Service desk and book a car to Pattaya. Tell them your hotel is …...". All bases covered, or so I hoped.

It transpired that I need not have worried. For once, Plan A went like clockwork. I was on time, his plane was on time and we had a comfortable, incident-free trip to Pattaya. The hotel check-in completed, I suggested we should go for a wander to give my friend a brief orientation and let him familiarize himself with a few of the nearer drinking establishments. Alas, it was late and he was tired. He pointed out that he had lost three hours on the plane trip over, so he needed to adjust. I replied that he should not worry about it because he will get the three hours back on the plane trip home. He was not in a humorous mood, so we arranged to meet the following day at 2:00pm, this being the usual time that Pattaya residents wake from their alcohol-induced slumber. Not much happens in Pattaya before this hour anyway.

The next day, at 2:00pm, I found him sitting in the foyer of his hotel. He did not look very happy so I inquired as to what was wrong. I thought there may have been a problem with the hotel or his room. "Don't ask", he stated glibly. Now of course, as soon as anyone tells you not to ask, what do you do? He still wouldn't tell me so I threatened to hold my breath until he did.

"You're going to think I'm an idiot."
I was about to reply, "what's the 'going to' bit?" but decided to bite my tongue until I heard his story.

His night's sleep was good but, unfortunately, he was still suffering from jetlag and his body clock decided he should get up at the unheard of hour of 10:00am. With nothing to do and four hours to do it in, he decided to venture out on his own to discover the 'real' Thailand. If we had had more time together I could have told him he would never find the 'real' Thailand here in Pattaya. But the hotel kindly provided a free

Pattaya map with the location of his hotel clearly marked 'you are here' and he wanted to play adventurer. Being somewhat hungry, his first task was to look for a good Thai restaurant where he could try authentic Thai food. He was quite partial to hot and spicy food as long as it was not at the furnace stage.

After leaving the hotel it only took a two hundred metre walk before, as luck would have it, he found what he was looking for. In fact, luck had nothing to do with it because if you walked anywhere around Pattaya and did not find a Thai restaurant within two hundred meters it would be astounding.

He sat at an empty table and the waiter approached with the menu – all in Thai, except for a smattering of English words here and there. He glanced at the page and picked out what English he could decipher.

"Is this one chicken?" he asked. A nod and a smile affirmed his guess. No, on second thoughts, I don't feel like chicken.

"What about this one? Is the pork fried or barbecued?" Another nod confirmed that the waiter could not understand a word he said. Pointing to the next item he simply asked, "Fish?" Much nodding and smiling. And so it went on, the pointing, the smiling and the waiter, with pencil and paper in hand, nodding enthusiastically. Finally he decided he did want chicken after all. He moved his finger back to his first choice and handed the menu back to the grinning waiter who then retreated to the kitchen.

It was about then he noticed that the three Thais sitting at the next table were laughing and, not too subtly, looking his way. Let them laugh, he mused. If they came to my country and could not speak the language I would probably be laughing at them too.

Five minutes later a beaming waitress arrived with a hot dish and placed it before him. This is fish, not chicken. Never mind. It looked and smelled delicious so he was not going to argue the point. With fork and spoon in hand he was about to take his first mouthful when the waitress returned with another steaming hot plate. This time it *was* chicken. Two? Confused, he again decided not to protest but try his two course meal instead. Next came a large bowl of boiled rice. That's ok. One cannot have a meal in Asia without rice. Then came another dish, this time barbecued chicken. Then another ...and another. All in all, eight plates of food appeared on his table, plus the one bowl of rice. With his mouth agape, the laughter from his Thai neighbours was now clearly audible and understandable.

"I didn't order all this," he protested.
The waiter, smiling and nodding, took out his notepad and pointed to the page with eight lines of Thai writing on it.
"You order."
The penny dropped with a thud that could be heard clear across the Pacific. While my friend had merely been questioning the items on the menu, the waiter had been merrily noting each one down as his order. My friend decided to accept his fate rather than look more foolish than he already felt.

Unable to control myself any longer, the tears welled up in my eyes as I burst with laughter.
"What did you do?" was all I could get out.
"I pretended it was what I wanted and that I was a food-taster," much as a food connoisseur or food critic would sample the delights of a restaurant before writing a review in *Pigs Monthly*.
"The bill came to six hundred *baht*."
With my speech still impaired by laughter, I could not resist.
"Why didn't you ask for a doggy bag?"
"Fuck off!"

14

Tangled Web

Ever had the feeling that you are about to make a terrible mistake? It is that feeling that comes from deep inside your gut but is triggered by long-slumbering cells in some dark corner of your brain. These cells recall similar incidents from your recent past or childhood and send up a red neon banner flashing the words "Warning! Warning!" Then that little voice inside your head shouts, "Hey, moron! Remember the last time you did something like this? Remember what happened?" Finally comes that other little voice saying, "No, this time it is different. This time I'll be careful. I won't make the same mistake again." Then you do.

The nature of man is that he just cannot help himself. Worse is the fact that he cannot help himself where women are concerned. Don't ever listen to those people who preach that it's a man's world. Women have the power and tragically, they know how to use it. Their greatest weapon is their ability to let men *think* they are in control. Pattaya is a prime example. On the surface you would think Pattaya is the ultimate man's world, a playground for men because they wield their power through money. In reality, it is the bar girls who are in total control and they pull the strings as artfully as any master puppeteer.

This story is about some seriously clever manipulation. I would like to say that it was on my part but alas, I was on the receiving end. It all began some time ago in the Chinese Year of the Idiot. I had been living with my girlfriend for eighteen months and all was well. The circumstance of our meeting is a story in itself, 'Fa-lung For Sale', but suffice to say that as far as Thai girlfriends go, she was great. She never asked for anything, worked long hours in a restaurant to help support us and basically loved me to death. The latter was her first mistake because I began to feel I was being smothered. Her only other mistake was, because she worked until midnight every night, I was left to my own devices. In Pattaya, the mind of any man left alone at night is a devil's playground and he was about to have a lot of fun with mine.

I met a girl in a bar. Actually, I met two girls in the same bar. The first was the subject of another story, 'Reality Check', and the second was offered to me on a silver platter. Her name was *Pom*, she was eighteen and had never worked in a bar before. The *mamasan* told me this girl had liked me from the first time she saw me but had kept in the background because my attentions were focused on the other lady. Now that the association with lady number one had ended, she wanted me to know she was there for me. Besides that, she liked older men. "Warning! Warning! You have just been fed a total crock." These are the words that pounded throughout every fibre of my being but, true to form, my second little voice drowned them out by saying, "God, but she's beautiful." Sense and sensibility – nil; ego and stupidity – 1.

My new admirer told me she only worked as cashier (Warning! Warning!) and was not available to be bar fined. I know she had plenty of offers but I never saw her go with another *fa-lung*. Every night I would go to her bar at the 5:00pm opening time and stay until very late. My girlfriend started to get suspicious because I was continually arriving home at two or three in the morning. I countered by saying that I was out drinking with my friends and playing snooker. Whether she believed that or not, I did not care.

What follows is a classic tale in that I was the proud recipient of the full Pattaya treatment. "I love you welly much" ; "I can everything for you" ; "I miss you too much" and "You number one for me." As though I've never heard that before. The next one, though, just blew me away.

"I never have man before. I virgin." Ok, I believed she worked as cashier, being the only girl there with any mathematical ability and I also knew she did like me because she never asked anything from me. She was not one of those 'you sit and buy me lady drinks all night' parasites. However, I found it difficult to believe a girl as beautiful as she was, had never had sex before the age of eighteen.

I started to crave and plan and scheme. I told a couple of close friends about the situation. "Do you believe her?" "I don't know, but I would love to find out." The consensus was that I should see it through to the end and, in truth, I could never forgive myself if I simply let her slip away. One close friend came to my aid. He had an apartment in Pattaya and was leaving soon so he kindly gave me permission to use it while he was away to enable me to consummate my relationship with *Pom*. This was a double bonus because my own place was totally off limits, not only for the obvious reason. My apartment was extremely primitive and, even if I was living alone, as soon as *Pom* saw it, she would correctly conclude I was a no-hoper and the relationship would certainly be over. My friend's apartment was luxurious and more importantly, located in a very secluded area. The chances of me being caught out were extremely remote. This meant I now had the perfect venue for my tryst.

Another problem arose. I have never 'been with' a virgin before. If everything she told me was the truth, then this was going to be my first time also. Back in my younger days I would pick girls up by telling them I was a fantastic lover, that I was extremely well endowed and that I could last all night and give them orgasm after orgasm. By the time they found out what an unmitigated liar I was, it was too late. The deed was done and I was lying back smoking a cigarette. With *Pom*, her inexperience meant the pressure was on me to perform. No more wham-bam-thank-you-mam.

The next problem was, since she worked as cashier, she was not available for bar fines. How then could I get her out of the place? One evening I decided to test it out by asking *mamasan* if I could take *Pom* to the movies for a couple of hours. *Mamasan* said Ok. I then asked if

I had to pay the bar fine for her to leave the bar. "No. She no bar fine. Go with you Ok." Success. I checked the movie start times and the following night at 8:00pm, walked out of the bar with *Pom*.

At this point I should explain that Pattaya is a very small place. Everyone knows everyone else's business and basically, you cannot get away with very much here. I thought that taking my new love to the movies was pretty safe – until I sat down in the theatre. The house lights were still on and sitting directly in front of me was a girl I had known for some years. She worked at a bar in *soi* 8 and knew my girlfriend. Every girl working at that bar also knew my girlfriend. I was caught red handed. We exchanged pleasantries and I sank lower in my seat as I quietly prayed that she would turn out to be the only bar girl in Pattaya who could keep her mouth shut. Once the movie finished, I quickly returned *Pom* to her bar in safe, sound and pristine condition.

Yet another problem raised its ugly head and I mean that literally. Why is it every gorgeous girl in the world, no matter what nationality, always has one ugly friend? *Pom* was no exception. Her friend was totally unattractive to the extent that I never knew whether to talk to her or saddle her. The friend was also very protective of *Pom*. I eventually made my move and asked *Pom* if she wanted to go with me. Her enthusiasm at the idea left me in no doubt that she really did like me, however there was one catch. There always is. *Pom* spoke to *mamasan* about it and *mamasan* said ok, but the horse would have to come along as chaperone. The thought of spending the night with *Pom* was exciting to say the least, but to say the idea of sharing the nuptial bed with Trigger was a downer is like saying that Everest is a small hill. Another challenge to face - how to get *Pom* alone. *Mamasan* greedily suggested that I bar fine the two of them. This was the first time the words 'bar fine' were mentioned as far as *Pom* was concerned. Was I making progress or merely getting to the truth of the matter?

The solution came from an unexpected source. I had decided that a night without *Pom* was worse than sharing a bed with an ugly woman. I went to my friend's apartment to make sure all was ready, that the manager did not have any problem with the arrangement and the night security guard knew my face well enough not to shoot me if I approached the building at 2:00am. All was fine until the manager asked me how many people would be staying the night. I replied three, myself and two ladies. This was unacceptable. It was fine for me to stay plus one lady, if I gave them a photocopy of her ID card beforehand. At the time I realized this was not such a bad thing. He was responsible for the security of the apartments and if I, a non-paying guest, started bringing back a stream of bar girls for overnighters, he would be in trouble should something go missing or if there was a problem. Thinking about it again, I realized it was a great idea. I could now do something totally foreign to me and tell *Pom* and *mamasan* the truth. I was only allowed to take one girl back and the other would have to remain in her stable. Problem solved.

On hearing the news *Pom* did look sincerely disappointed. When told, the horse looked totally downtrodden. She had just lost her only chance to ever be bar fined. Frantic Thai conversation ensued with the result that we were at a stalemate. I would not be allowed to bar fine *Pom* without taking her companion also. Simple as that.

Yes, I could have booked at room at a hotel, bought some sleeping pills, taken them both back to the room and drugged Mister Ed. I thought seriously about it but I really did not want it to be like that. I wanted it to be more romantic. And yes, as much as I fought against it and as much as I denied it, I was beginning to think about *Pom* as more than just a one-night stand.

What is it about men that they desire most that which they can not have. I read this years ago and did not believe a word of it. I have always liked things easy, the easier the better. Whenever the going got tough, I gave up. But now here I was in Pattaya where I could easily have any one of the thousands of pretty bar girls, yet the only one I wanted was *Pom*.

The next evening *Pom* informed me that Mama and Papa were arriving the following day for a visit and to make sure she was happy in her new job. The fact that their visit coincided with *Pom*'s payday did strike me as being more than mere chance. She had also told her parents about me and they wanted to meet me, presumably to check me out as well. This felt a little strange as I thought my days of meeting parents and seeking their approval to go out with their daughter were well and truly over. It has been my experience over the years that the parents of the girls I went out with never liked me very much. The really frightening thought running through my mind was, given *Pom*'s age, I was probably older than both of them. I considered not showing up and later making up some pathetic excuse as to why.

But I did show up and yes, I was older than them. I made my *sawatdee's*, smiled a lot and back-peddled as much as possible so as to avoid being asked any questions. From a safe distance I noticed them occasionally looking my way, probably sizing me up in terms of a new roof, refrigerator or TV.

Yet another issue occurred to me. Should I be successful in extracting *Pom* from the clutches of the bar and should we have a romantic night together, what do I do the next morning? She always stated that she was "not same lady bar" and kept telling me how much she loved me, so where did that leave me? Do I give her money or what? If it were known around town that she was a virgin and available, she could easily demand 10,000 *baht* for the first night. There was no way I could afford that kind of money. What if the next morning she did ask me for money? It would immediately shatter my illusions and reduce our relationship to a common everyday business arrangement. What if I offered her money and she took offence? If everything she said were true and she really was 'not same lady bar', it would be a gross insult to cheapen our relationship to a purely financial one.

This was my headache and I did not know how to solve it. Yes, I could tell her to stop work and I would take care of her in the future. But it all came down to money. I had none. Secondly, it would not be easy for me to extract myself from my existing relationship. I still have a conscience and the thought of kicking my girlfriend out simply because I had found someone younger and prettier would make me feel lower than shark shit.

78

They say life is supposed to get easier as you get older. The more you experience, the more you learn, the more you know and the easier things become. Life in Pattaya is supposed to be easier still. Girls, love and sex available on tap, to be turned on and off at will. In my case this is not so. There are things I think I know and there are things that I think I have learned but, when it comes to the crunch, I am just as stupid as I ever was. The words from Bon Jovi ,"gonna take a miracle to save you this time", kept repeating in my head. I prayed for divine intervention.

The days passed and my frustration grew. I kept telling *Pom* I could not take two ladies back to the apartment. *Pom* kept telling me she wanted to go with me and the friend kept insisting she had to come along. Finally, I made the decision to bite the bullet and, come hell or high water, tonight was going to be the night. I would bar fine the two of them and felt sure that I could sneak them past the security guard. *Pom* was ecstatic but the friend did not look too happy about it. Maybe she was just in a bad mood. There is nothing worse than an ugly woman in an ugly mood.

Twenty-eight years ago, a few mates and I would get together and go out on the town, visiting pubs, clubs and discos with the view to picking up girls. Even though we wore the trendiest gear, used the best lines and knew the latest dance steps, we invariably ended the night going home drunk and alone. We coined a name for such nights – *unfucking*. During my university years I had many *unfucking* nights.

Now, a quarter of a century later, I stumbled upon the Pattaya version of this unique game. Playing '*Unfucking*, Pattaya Style' is simple. All you have to do is bar fine two girls at the same time, one of whom does not have sex while the other probably would consent to sex but she is so far down on your list of 'Sexual Experiences I Must Have Before I Die', that she slots in immediately after 'Smashing my testicles between two house bricks'. Then you sleep, fully clothed, with both of them in the one bed and listen to them snore all night. In the morning, you wake up with lovers' balls so bad that the ugly one starts to look good. How do I know this? Because that is exactly what I did.

15

Ko Something

I am an adventurer - a born traveler. The blood of Magellan, Cook and Livingstone courses through my veins. As most residents of Pattaya will testify, merely waking up every afternoon is an adventure in itself. When the first photons of light fight their way through engorged blood vessels to my slumbering retina, my first conscious thought is always, "Where am I?" followed immediately by, "Who the hell are you?"

Needless to say, I do try to limit my adrenaline rushes to just one or two per day. In this respect, I do not get in or on any velocipede that does not have wheels. Furthermore, I do not get in or on any moving object whose total sum of wheels is not evenly divisible by four or six. This eliminates horses, motorcycles, tricycles, elephants and, more to the point, boats. The fact I am alive and well to this day can be attributed to my adherence to this hard and fast rule.

Alas, like all hard and fast rules, I've been known to break them occasionally. It happened that I was invited to go with a group of friends to a place I had never heard of before. This is not unusual. I am often invited, by friends and strangers alike, to go to places I have never heard of, probably in the hope that I won't be able to find my way back. I did not ask where it was because I am very protective of my ignorance. The name still escapes me, so let's call it *Ko* Something. My girlfriend comes from *Korat* so, at the time, I guessed it must be near there, seeing that both names started with '*Ko*'.

On the morning of departure I was surprised to find my friends turn up at my apartment carrying an excess of aquatic and beach paraphernalia. *Korat*, as I remembered, was nowhere near the beach, so geography theory number one went out the window. At least the hired minibus had four wheels. "Get in! We're late!"

After driving for what seemed an eternity, we arrived at a small beachside hamlet. The gear was unpacked from the vehicle and my companions headed for the beach. Oh well, this must be the *Ko* place. A nice day at the seaside, I can handle that. It was only when I noticed them all pointing out across that large expanse of blue wet stuff that panic set in. It was then I realized what the word '*Ko*' meant. It meant 'island'. As my pals merrily skipped towards a very large piece of driftwood by the water's edge, my legs turned to jelly and my life, as miserable as it has been, swept past my eyes to add just one more torture to the day.

The large piece of driftwood turned out to be a boat. The definition of the word 'boat' in my dictionary is 'a floatation device used for transporting people or goods over water'. Well, this big log was apparently going to attempt to traverse water. The floatation bit was highly debatable. As for transporting people, that looked out of the question. The boat was long and thin and looked as if it would sit very low in the water. Were all five of us supposed to get in this suspect floating tree trunk? Unfortunately the answer was yes.

The crew was a man in his late hundreds wearing only a pair of shorts that were even older than he was. His skin was leathery and dark, but not dark enough to hide the grizzly tattoos on his upper arms and back. A large cylindrical piece of paper stuck out of his mouth as if to defy gravity. A second glance revealed it was actually conical in shape, with the thin end stuck in his mouth as if super-glued to his bottom lip. The wider end was covered in grey ash. It looked like he was sucking a small ice cream cone.

As a concession to the twentieth century, the boat was motor driven. The engine consisted of a round lump of rusty, oily metal down at the blunt end of the tree trunk. The engine was sitting on a long shaft with a wooden handle. Protruding from the other end was a long shaft with what passed as a propeller at one end. Balanced on a makeshift bench was a large plastic bottle containing a pinkish liquid. I estimated the bottle would hold about twenty litres. A thin plastic tube ran from a hole through the lid to the lump of rusty metal.

I looked out across the water. There was a smudge on the horizon that appeared to be our destination. I remembered from my school days that the horizon, when viewed across water, is about twenty miles away. Therefore, the maximum distance I would have to swim in the event of certain tragedy was ten miles. I can't walk that far. I quickly looked around for anything that looked like it would float. Something I could utilize if I needed to tread water – life jackets, drinking containers, air bags, plastic bags, straws....

My friends appeared unconcerned about the lack of safety features of our intended transportation as they nudged me out of my trancelike state to help stow the gear on board. The captain of the Titanic sat near the engine just watching, smiling and smoking his ice cream cone. Once the gear was all aboard, he directed us to push the log away from the beach.

"Isn't this fun?" one of my friends remarked as we strained with the heavier boat. I forced a smile to hide the fact I was wishing the bloody thing would remain on the sandy bottom and be swamped. But it didn't happen. To my amazement it actually floated, even after the five well-fed foreigners scrambled aboard.

The Thai captain pulled on a rope and the engine began to splutter. Once more and a cloud of black smoke signalled that it was up and running. He manoeuvred the large stick so the end with the propeller rested under the water and we were on our way. He looked very pleased with himself as he sat on the wooden bench seat near the engine and steered the boat towards our island destination.

We were about at the halfway mark when I noticed Captain Ahab stand and affix a rope to the steering stick. The rope was tied at both ends to opposite sides of the boat and had a loop in the middle. He placed the loop over the stick and sat down. This was the auto pilot. The craft, presumably, would now head in a straight line with the Captain left hands-free.

He smiled as he removed a small piece of paper from a plastic bag he had stored near his feet. He then produced another plastic bag that appeared to contain a very suspicious leafy brown substance. I was hoping it was tobacco. With his hands in his lap so I could not quite get a clear view of exactly what he was doing, his decades of experience enabled him to roll what passed for a cigarette within a matter of seconds. Unlike the factory-made version, it was conical in shape and looked exactly like the miniature ice cream cone that I had seen him sucking on earlier.

While my friends continued to watch the featureless ocean about them and drown their lilly-white bodies in the ample sunshine, I watched the old man of the sea. He looked down at the wooden seat, dug his fingernail under a piece of the timber and broke off a splinter about ten centimetres long. With the cigarette glued to his lips and the wooden splinter in one hand, he carefully unscrewed the top of the large plastic bottle, making sure that the tube remained submerged in the liquid as he removed the lid. He then dunked the stick in the liquid, giving it a good soaking before removing it.

Totally intrigued, I watched as he swivelled around and leant toward the engine. Disconnecting the wire from the spark plug, he held it with one hand about a centimetre from the plug. With his other hand he placed the petrol-doused splinter of wood between the contacts and allowed the ensuing sparks to ignite it. The engine gave a splutter or two but, unconcerned, he quickly reconnected the spark plug lead.

The stick was burning fiercely as he brought it up to his cigarette, took a few puffs and, satisfied that it was alight, threw the burning stick over the side. All this happened in a few seconds, such was his skill.

Turning around, he calmly screwed the lid back on the plastic bottle of highly flammable liquid.

My friends never saw any of the old man's antics. As he puffed away, I sat in amazement and pictured the *Bangkok Post* headlines: "Five foreigners incinerated in fireball. Body parts found as far away as Singapore."

Much to my surprise, we made it to our destination and spent the day swimming, diving, frolicking and devouring our pre-packed lunch. I spent much of the time looking for a convenience store on what was a largely uninhabited island.

When we finally had our fill of sun, sea and sand, it was time for the boat trip back to civilization. Being experienced sailors by now, it took no time at all to re-pack our gear into the boat. Just before he got into the boat to allow the passengers the privilege of pushing the vessel off the sand, I approached the captain. He smiled in puzzled gratitude as I handed him a gift - a brand new, recently-purchased cigarette lighter.

16

Music to My Ears

It should not take visitors to Pattaya very long to realize that this city has an anthem. It is a song played every day in almost every bar across town and has become very well known by locals and tourists alike. 'Hotel California', easily the most recognizable of 'The Eagles' hits, is a good song but I admit to being sick of hearing it. I have a friend who has the dangerous habit of requesting the song each time he goes to a bar where there is a band playing. He only does it to annoy people but, one day, he is going to be severely injured.

But should it be the anthem of Pattaya? What does a song about an American insane asylum have to do with Pattaya? Sorry I asked. I would have thought that another of 'The Eagles' hits would be more appropriate:

"...you can't hide your Lying Eyes."

This made me think about offering possible alternatives for a new Anthem of Pattaya. What about Roxette's, 'Joyride' which begins:

"Hello, you fool, I love you,
C'mon join the joyride."

Even old Elvis Presley hits such as 'His Latest Flame'

"...would you believe, that yesterday,
that girl was in my arms and swore to me,
she'd be mine eternally?
And Marie's (Lek's) the name,
of his latest flame."

and 'Devil In Disguise' come to mind:

"She looks like an angel,
Walks like an angel,
Talks like an angel'
But I got wise.
She's the devil in disguise."

Or what about the sultry Marilyn Munroe warning us all many years ago that
"...A kiss may be grand but it won't pay the rental,
Diamonds are a girl's best friend."

And let's not forget The Beatles' classic 'Can't Buy Me Love'. With so many choices, it is difficult to decide which one typifies the true soul of Pattaya.

With or without an anthem, music does play a major role in the daily life of Pattaya and there is a plethora of bars catering to music enthusiasts. The problem in the ordinary Beer Bars is not the quantity or variety of music on offer, but the auditory challenge of listening to a half dozen different songs being played simultaneously at aircraft engine sound levels. The conclusion drawn is that Thais believe the louder and more unintelligible the noise, like moths to a flame, the more customers will be attracted to it. This of course is nonsense, but many a foreign bar owner has seen the folly of trying to change the Thai system.

Country music, pop music, 'techno' crap and Rock 'n Roll bars are easy to find. Many will play requests and allow customers to pick and choose what they wish to listen to. Some, however, set conditions.

One bar advises that, "If you want to hear 'Back Street Boys', fuck off." The staff can also be very selective and unforgiving about the type of music they want to listen to. One Go Go Bar owner had two of his dancing maidens quit because they said that they could not dance to the music he was playing. What could he do? He liked the music, more importantly his customers liked the music, but it cost him two of his star attractions.

On the other hand, every bar owner knows that the fastest way to clear a bar of customers is to play Thai music. The girls will love it, singing along and dancing to the rhythm, but that is not going to generate income for the bar. The paying customers will not understand the lyrics and the staff may take more notice of the music than a *fa-lung* in need of attention. Personally, I like Thai music. Not the traditional stuff, but the pop songs sung by bands like 'Loso', 'Fly' and artists like 'Bird'.

Unfortunately, and I am loathe to place this in the category of 'music', mention should be made of that most accursed of Japanese inventions, the Karaoke Bar. Exclusively Thai Karaoke Bars are plentiful and should be avoided at all costs. Unfortunately, some catering for foreigners have sprung up and only go to prove that ninety-nine point nine percent of humanity cannot sing. One hundred percent of drunk humanity cannot sing. The main purpose of these dens must surely be to promote the Frank Sinatra hit, 'My Way', and if I ever hear that song again it will be too soon. When are the authorities going to introduce a law that the exterior walls of all Karaoke Bars be made from soundproof material?

But returning to my quest for an anthem, Pattaya already has a song written about it. I don't know the name – I just call it 'The Pattaya Song' – but it is sung in English and has a lively calypso beat. The entertainers at Malibu Bar on the corner of *Soi* Post Office and Second Road mime and dance to it at the finale of their show. It is easy listening but the words are just not quite right.

I was forced to go back to the 1969 musical comedy *Paint Your Wagon*, starring Lee Marvin, Clint Eastwood and Jean Seberg, to find the most appropriate song for the Anthem of Pattaya. The song which has stayed in my mind is titled, 'The Gospel of No Name City' and was sung by the fire-and-brimstone preacher in the movie. From memory, the lyrics are as follows and, if I had to choose a song to be Pattaya's new anthem, this would be it.

"If you want to see sin of the wickedest kind,
Here it is.
You want to see virtue left behind,
Here it is.
Sodom was vice and vice versa,
You want to see where the vice is worser,
Here it is.
I mean here it is.

"You want to live life in the rottenest way,
Here it is.
Women and whisky night and day,
Here it is.
You want to embrace the Golden Calf,
Ankle and thigh and upper half,
Here it is.
I mean here it is."

17

Hello 'ello 'ello

In the book *Money Number One*, I briefly recounted an incident that brought the relationship with my first ever Thai girlfriend to an abrupt end. I mentioned that she 'cost me a fortune but taught me many valuable lessons'. Now it is time to tell, in more detail, the saga of our relationship and in particular, its untimely demise.

I had already spent a total of three days and four nights in Bangkok before arriving in Pattaya. I fell in love with the place from the moment I arrived and was having the time of my life. There was no desire at all to go back to Bangkok.

I'm not going to shock you by saying I met her in a bar, nor am I going to surprise you by admitting that I was three sheets to the wind at the time. Nevertheless, at two thirty in the morning, when I checked bin, I paid her bar fine as well. At least she could help me navigate back to my hotel. I don't remember much of that trip and I believe I was unconscious before I even hit the pillow so, in bar girl terms, she had an easy night.

The next morning I awoke to find a naked girl in my bed and, with no hint of the expected hangover, decided to take full advantage of the situation. She had a beautiful body although her face left a bit to be desired. I'm no oil painting myself. A bout of bedroom exercise and then it was back to sleep. We woke mid-afternoon, showered and dressed, but before she left there was the little matter of business to take care of. "One thousand *baht*." Nowadays I only ever pay five hundred *baht* and would scoff at any suggestion that I pay one thousand *baht* for a night with a girl from a Beer Bar. To me, sex is sex - sometimes good, sometimes better. But on no account could I ever say that one girl was twice as good as another and therefore warranted to be paid double the fee. Back in my novice days, things were different and, without my current rationale to guide me, money was not a consideration.

That evening I again found myself with nothing to do and eventually gravitated back to her bar. No sooner had I sat down than the *mamasan* approached me.
"Your lady. She come. Half hour."
My lady? Where do you get this "your lady" bit? I was a little confused but, sure enough, in less than thirty minutes *Nong* appeared and made a beeline straight for me.

And so it was that I paid her bar fine for the remaining five nights of my stay. She told me she lived alone in an apartment and, every afternoon, would return to her room to change clothes, do her washing then meet me back at my hotel at 8:00pm. This was quite a convenient arrangement for me as it meant I had plenty of time to myself to explore and generally do my own thing. I must admit I had a great time with *Nong* on this, my first trip to Thailand. On the day of my departure there was a hint of a tear in her eyes and I promised I would come back as soon as I could.

Four weeks later I kept my promise. By the time I reached Pattaya it was 9:00pm so I directed the taxi driver to *Nong's* bar before checking in to my hotel. I was hoping to get to her before some other guy bar fined her. As it happened, I was in luck. She leapt towards the road as she saw me alight from the taxi and smothered me with hugs and kisses. I handed her enough money for five days of bar fines and she promptly gave it to the cashier. After a few quick "goodbye's" and some 'high-five's' to the other girls, she grabbed her purse and her toothbrush then hopped into the taxi for the trip to my hotel.

The time spent with *Nong* on this trip was as good as the first time but, in retrospect, there were a few subtle warning signs I should have heeded. For starters, her requests for money became more frequent. Even though she was no longer asking for one thousand *baht* per night to stay with me, I have since calculated she had actually cost me more.

Every day I would be told "I not like work bar", suggesting of course that I should support her. (When our relationship was over, I found out she had been working in that same bar for six years so for a girl who did "not like work bar', she certainly was a masochist.) There was also the, "have no money pay room". She even brought the invoice along to show me. Like a fool, I fell straight into that one. What the hell, it was only 2,500 *baht*. (Again, I discovered later I was not the only *fa-lung* paying her rent.)

A few months later, on my third trip to Pattaya, I took her to her home in *Kam Paeng Phet*. She was now costing me much more than one thousand *baht* per day because I was supporting her totally. She told me she had finished working in the bar. (Not really true.)

We arrived back in Pattaya in the late afternoon and went straight to my hotel. *Nong* then said she would take her things to her room and come back at the usual time of eight o'clock. I told her, "I'll come with you. I want to see your apartment." Well, it was like I had just run over her grandmother and raped her cat!
"You cannot come apartment me. I never take *fa-lung* apartment me." With that, she walked out and I did not see her for the rest of the day.

Next morning she came to my room, apologized and said if I still wanted to see her apartment, I could. It did not take an Einstein to work out that whatever it was that she did not want me to see had now been removed and her room had been made 'safe' for me to look over. I went anyway, to ensure I knew exactly where the apartment was.

I was very suspicious after that and would arrive at her apartment without giving her any warning. One day, instead of waiting for her to come to the hotel at 8:00pm as usual, I turned up at her apartment at 7:00pm. She had just showered, was dressing very quickly and I noticed she was in a particular hurry to leave. The bathroom door was also closed. She finished dressing but before she ushered me out of her room, I made the excuse that I needed to go to the toilet. In spite of her protestations, I headed towards the bathroom.

As I opened the door I felt a spongy resistance as it swung towards the wall. It was as if something very elastic or very rubbery was preventing the door from opening its full extent. This required some further investigation and when I looked behind the door, have a guess what I found? A spongy, rubbery, naked, wet Thai man squeezing himself deeper into the corner. Before I could say anything, the strangest thing happened. He raised his hand to his mouth, placed his index finger vertically across his lips and whispered, "Shhhhhh...". I burst into laughter. What in God's name was he thinking? To this day I cannot imagine what must have been going through his tiny little mind to allow him to make such an absurd gesture.

"Hello 'ello 'ello! What a surprise!" I exclaimed as I closed the bathroom door behind me. *Nong* said nothing as she stood utterly dejected in the centre of the room. As I walked past her to the front door, I merely made the comment, "I hope you like working bar" and left.

Over the next month I found out that the guy was her boyfriend/pimp with whom she had been living for three years. He was a motorcycle taxi driver who would also send her 'customers' from time to time. There were probably many other *fa-lung* also paying the rent for that enterprising bastard.

"Hello 'ello 'ello!"

18

Baht Bus Mafia

*B*aht Buses, also called *Baht* Taxis or '*rot sorng tair-o*' (literally "car two rows", describing the two bench seats in the back), are the dark blue converted Isuzu, Toyota, Nissan and Mitsubishi pickups that roam the streets of Pattaya in search of tired tourists and pedestrians. As the city's predominant form of mass public transport, they are an efficient and cheap means of getting around. I don't think anyone really knows how many *baht* buses prowl the streets of Pattaya, but I can assure you, there are enough.

After being here a while, you may notice that one of the most annoying sights for a *baht* bus driver to see is a *fa-lung* walking. It seems to really irritate them. Stroll along any of Pattaya's newly-paved but rapidly-deteriorating footpaths and each passing driver will beep the horn to signal that he is ready and more than willing to pick you up. And on the two-way streets, it is not just the ones going in your direction. The ones going the opposite way will also let out a blast. How on earth they could possibly believe that you are only walking north because you have an urgent desire to catch a taxi going south is beyond me.

One conclusion to draw is that the local Thai population do not enjoy walking. They appear only to walk as a last resort or if they do not have the funds to utilize a form of transportation. I once noticed a young Thai woman get on a taxi only to alight forty metres further down the road. She had no obvious physical handicap, it was close to sundown so the weather was not too hot and it was not raining. I can only conclude she was either in a desperate hurry or her shoes were hurting.

Unfortunately, *baht* buses have also figured prominently in the list of complaints made by foreigners, both tourists and expats alike. For many years now, Pattaya's English language newspapers have printed letters from disgruntled foreigners with accusations of being ripped off by *baht* bus drivers. Many complaints to the Tourist Police have been about the same matter. The problem was that the fare for travel anywhere within Pattaya City area was set at five *baht* per person but foreigners, particularly tourists, were consistently being charged ten or twenty *baht* per person. While many simply accepted there was a *'fa-lung* price' and a 'Thai price', others recognized this as a form of extortion.

The problem was eventually solved using typical Thai ingenuity. Now displayed inside each vehicle is a sign stating, "The regular fare of mini bus in Pattaya is not over 10 *baht* per person according to the law of enforced by the Department of Land Transport". The solution was to simply double the fare. But, (and here is the cunning bit), due to the generosity, benevolence and gooey-gooey niceness of Pattaya's *baht* taxi drivers, they still charge their Thai passengers only five *baht*. No longer are foreigners expected to pay double fare simply because they are foreigners. They now pay the correct fare and Thai people are given a 50% discount. Of course, if you happen to be traveling with a Thai companion, he or she will also be required to pay the correct fare so that the driver can be seen to be evenhanded and not because he knows you will be paying for your friend's trip anyway.

Tourists are often advised to negotiate any fares beforehand when traveling within a foreign country. This is good advice and is generally true. For travel on a *baht* bus within the confines of Pattaya City, once you understand the system, this is not really necessary. Newcomers should study a map and quickly familiarize themselves with the routes the buses take. You will quickly realize that the routes rarely vary and, even if they do, simply get off the *Baht* Bus, pay the fare and catch another one heading in the direction you wish to go.

Riding on a *baht* bus from South Pattaya to Naklua, I had my ten *baht* coin out to pay the fare. This is quite some distance so ten *baht* is the correct fare. Opposite *Soi* 7, along Pattaya Second Road, the car stopped to pick up more passengers. A *fa-lung* with his Thai girlfriend approached the driver and started to negotiate the fare to the Dusit Hotel. The *fa-lung* bargained the driver down to forty *baht* for the trip and looked pleased with himself as he and his girlfriend took their seats. I noted the Thai girl did not say a word to help her companion out even though she would certainly have known the correct fare. If he had consulted a map, all the guy needed to know was whether the taxi was going straight ahead at the Central Road intersection. All taxis heading that way pass the roundabout at the Pattaya North Road intersection and that is right outside the Dusit Hotel. There was no need to negotiate beforehand and the correct fare for the two of them should have been five *baht* each.

But it is still possible for *fa-lung* to succeed in paying the five *baht* 'Thai price' on the *baht* taxis. You may wonder why bother trying to save a paltry five *baht*. Well, it is not the money, it is the principle. I refuse to pay double price simply because I am a foreigner and they *think* I can afford it. Even though I am only the mouse in this game of cat and mouse, I employ several strategies which, to date, have been effective.

Firstly, I avoid getting on a *baht* bus that does not already have passengers on it, particularly Thai passengers. Many local Thais avoid this too, which is a fair indication that it is not a good idea. I believe the reasoning behind it is that the driver may demand a higher fare by saying he made a special trip for you and taken you somewhere he had not intended to go. If you are the only passenger and the driver stops to ask where you want to go, pay him the five *baht* and get off.

Secondly, I avoid getting on a *baht* bus where there is a woman sitting in the front passenger seat. She may simply be a passenger but often she is the driver's wife, girlfriend or mother who seems a lot happier with the two-tiered pricing system and more willing to argue with passengers than the driver, who is otherwise occupied.

Next, I always carry a lot of small change with me, particularly five *baht* coins. It is surprising just how many drivers do not have change for 20, 50 or 100 *baht* notes. If you hand over a ten *baht* coin, you will definitely not receive any change. When I get to where I want to go, I press the buzzer as late as possible so the taxi stops a short distance past my destination. I then place the exact fare into the driver's hand, turn around, check for traffic and walk back to my destination. I don't look at him or ask how much he wants. I don't ask if the fare is correct. I don't talk, discuss, argue or barter. At this point, should he want to question the fare, he will have to either leave the vehicle or reverse against the flow of traffic. The drivers very rarely do this, especially if there are other passengers in the vehicle. If he does chase me for extra money, I apologize politely and pay the extra five *baht*. Never, ever argue with a *baht* bus driver!

Finally, I avoid boarding the taxis that wait at supermarkets, shopping centres and bus stations, particularly those that park outside Royal Garden, Big C and the *Jomtien*-bound ones outside the school at South Pattaya. Even though they will certainly take you where you want to go, they sometimes charge as if for a private hire. Other times they may wait until they have a full load of passengers. This can take a while. You are better off walking past them and flagging down a taxi already in motion.

Using these tactics, I have had only two problems in four years of *baht* bus travel. The first was when I was playing tour guide for a friend recently arrived from Australia. I spent fifteen minutes explaining my game strategy to him before catching our first taxi. At our destination I told him to get off, walk away and not to look back while I settled the fare. I may as well have been speaking Swahili because, no sooner had I handed over the ten *baht* and begun my escape than my friend, facing the vehicle, gestured that the driver was calling me back. I uttered a four-letter obscenity and marvelled at my friend's lack of ability to follow simple instructions.

I have another friend, a long time visitor to Pattaya, who takes the game a little further. He has a collection of fifty *satang* and twenty-five *satang* coins and always keeps them in a separate pocket when he ventures out. These coins can only be found in your change at supermarkets or department stores and the general Thai population don't use them. He pays his fare with a five *baht* coin and if the driver begins to argue and demand the extra five *baht*, he apologizes and gladly offers to pay it. He then fumbles around in his pocket and takes his time counting out five *baht*'s worth of these small coins. Usually the drivers do not hang around but swear at him in Thai and drive off in disgust. Other times the drivers accept the money, swear at him in Thai and drive off in disgust.

Eventually, it reached the point where some of the drivers must have remembered him because he noticed they would not stop when he tried to flag them down. It did not matter because, with so many *baht* taxis about, it would take years before he offended every one of them. However, I do not recommend this practice. My friend has a very sick sense of humour.

I must know some really pathetic people because I have another friend who plays a much more dangerous game. Whenever the opportunity arises, he gets on a *baht* bus with a group of foreign tourists. If they get off anywhere near where he wants to go, he gets off with them, knowing full well they will overpay the fare. He just pretends to be part of the group and thus rides for free. This is very dangerous practice and I am sure people have been shot for lesser crimes than avoiding a five *baht* taxi fare.

Giving credit where credit is due, some drivers do charge their Thai passengers the ten *baht* fare. Whether this is through greed or a sense of fairness, I'll let you be the judge. One Thai man was very annoyed when he handed the driver a twenty *baht* note and only received ten *baht* change. Words were exchanged. The guy took note of the number of the taxi and, suffice to say, I would not like to be in that driver's shoes should he ever meet up with his disgruntled passenger in a dimly-lit area of Pattaya. As the only other passenger on the taxi at the time, I got the message and quickly exchanged the five *baht* coin in my hand for a ten *baht* coin in my pocket.

So, London may have the Underground, New York the Subway and Bangkok the Skytrain, but Pattaya has the *rot sorng tair-o*. They stop wherever they feel like it, block traffic, slow traffic, pollute the air and generally make up their own driving rules as they go along. Love them or hate them, it would be a sad day for Pattaya if they were ever taken out of service. Any alternative sanitized form of mass transit just would not have the character, be as economical nor be as much fun.

19

Fa-lung For Sale

W hat can I say? The relationship with my Long Term Thai Girlfriend Number Two ended while I was in Manila. Her name was *Mam* and she was a vast improvement on LTTG#1 except she had one major flaw. She had a gambling problem. It came to a head when she phoned me in Manila to say she had lost 10,000 *baht* playing cards. If she did not pay the money by the end of the month, all sorts of horrors would befall her. Could I send her the money. I replied in loud, slow English that I was not responsible for her gambling losses and I was not going to fund her addiction. She countered with "then I have to go back work bar, go with *fa-lung*". This attempt at making me jealous failed miserably and I ended the year-long love affair with the words, "Good. Let them pay for your losses". Click.

Three weeks later I was back in Pattaya. Newly single, I was determined to make the most of my freedom and be a 'butterfly', with no attachments nor involvement with any female other than sharing a bed for a few hours. This would be the perfect remedy for my slightly broken heart. This would also help me get over the anger. This was my plan.

The first night, a girl in *Soi* 9 took my fancy. The second, one in *Soi* 7. The third night I went drinking with some mates and when they finally called it a night at 2:00pm, I found myself at a bar in *Soi* 2, very drunk and very alone. I paid the bar fine for the girl who had been playing the dice game with me for a while. I should point out here that I am attracted to girls with long straight black hair, (am I in the right place or what?), so when I woke up the next morning to find the girl laying beside me had short, dyed-blonde wavy hair, I thought I was hallucinating. Where the hell did you come from? As the morning progressed, she appeared in no hurry to leave so I hastened things along by telling her she had to go because I was going to meet some friends. This worked. I paid her off and eased her out the door.

Walking back to the hotel later that afternoon, I decided to have one night off from butterflying. I would just spend a quiet evening in my room watching TV. No sooner had I picked up my key from reception than who should grab me but my short blonde curly-haired friend from the night before.
"What are you doing here?"
"I come see you. Stay with you."
"No you don't. Tonight I stay alone." This did not dissuade her and she followed me to my room.
"Look. You cannot stay. I'm tired and want to go to sleep."
"No problem. I sleep too."
Inside the room, I fired my final weapon. It had always proved a sure way to get rid of a bar girl.
"I have no money. I am not going to give you any money."
"No problem. I no want money. I love you."
Give me a break.

The next morning I again woke up beside Blondie and still did not know her name. Showering and dressing quickly, it was time for the "going to meet some friends" ploy that had been successful the previous day. She was a little more reluctant to leave this time so, contrary to my determination not to give her any money, I handed her two hundred *baht* saying it was for *gin kao*. Standing in the doorway she asked, "I come see you tonight?"
"No. I will be out most of the night. I will come to your bar."
"You come my bar?" she beamed.
"Yes," I lied. "Wait for me there."

With that she slowly walked off. I felt like a true bastard but what else could I do? I was not interested in becoming involved with another bar girl.

Alone in my room I realized that, when I did not show up at her bar that night, she would come looking for me. There seemed to be only one option. I packed my suitcase and checked out of the hotel.

Finding another hotel was not difficult due to the fact it was low season. I checked into a new place which was quite some distance from the previous hotel and more importantly, a long way from *soi* 2. I celebrated my re-acquired freedom with lunch and a swim at *Jomtien* and also decided tonight was going to be my night off from the women.

Returning to the hotel at around four in the afternoon, I was standing at the entrance when I noticed a familiar face. Walking past the hotel was a girl I had known for some time but had not seen for several months. She used to work in the bar with my card-playing ex-girlfriend and I had always liked her. She recognized me and stopped for a chat. She told me she had just broken up with her boyfriend with whom she had been living for six months. That explained why she quit work at the bar and why I hadn't seen her recently. He was a *fa-lung* working in *Rayong* and had recently decided he wanted a new girlfriend. She was back in Pattaya looking for a job and a room. She no longer wanted to work in a bar as she was a qualified masseuse and wanted to find work in a 'legitimate' massage parlour. I remembered she did give excellent neck and shoulder massages.

She had been looking for an apartment all day long only to find that most of the available ones were out of her price range.
"Do you have somewhere to stay tonight?" I asked.
"No have."
Sir Galahad to the rescue.
"Look, this is my hotel. I'm in room 205. Tonight I am staying alone. If you cannot find an apartment by say, ten o'clock, come back here. You are welcome to stay with me."
"You not have lady tonight?"

"No lady."
"What about *Mam*?"
"*Mam* and I finished."
"I sorry."
"I'm not."
"Thank you."
I went to my room, selfishly hoping she would not be able to find an apartment.

At exactly 10:00pm, the phone rang. She was calling from the hotel reception.
"You alone? You no have lady?"
"No lady. Come on up."
I could scarcely contain my joy. When she arrived at the door she really did look exhausted. I felt so sorry for her as she sadly sat on the bed and placed her small carry-bag containing one change of clothing on the floor beside her. In her hand was a well-thumbed notebook full of addresses and telephone numbers she had been given as possible contacts. I asked her if she was hungry and she lied that she had already eaten. I got her a soft drink and we sat and talked for an hour, about anything and everything. She wanted to know why *Mam* and I split up and I asked her about her ex-boyfriend. Eventually she looked at me with puppy-dog eyes and said, "You and me, same same." I suggested that she should go and have a nice, long, hot shower and then we could both get some sleep. In the morning, after breakfast, I told her I would help her look for an apartment. I knew some places too but, truthfully, I was enjoying her company.

She emerged from the bathroom, fully dressed in the same clothes as before. I switched off the light and still wearing my shorts and t-shirt, crawled into bed beside her. As we fell asleep you could have driven a tank through the space between us but I awoke in the morning with her head resting on my shoulder, her arm around me and her leg draped across mine. This was how I liked to sleep and obviously, she did too. We were both used to sleeping with a partner and at some point during the course of the night, had unconsciously gravitated towards each other. It felt great and I was happy.

We ate breakfast in the hotel café, then headed off apartment-hunting together. By lunchtime there was still no success and I realized, with me tagging along, enterprising apartment managers may have been inflating their prices, thinking that a *fa-lung* was paying. I suggested she continue the search without me and she agreed. I also asked that, whether she found a room or not, she come back to the hotel at six o'clock so we could go out for dinner and see a movie together. She thanked me and said she would like that very much. Before parting company, I pressed a thousand *baht* note into her hand.

"No. No. For what?" she protested.

"Look, I know you don't have a lot of money, so this may help."

She looked at me and sadly asked, "You know I have problem?"

"Yes, I know."

She threw her arms around me, whispered, "thank you", in my ear and set of to find a room.

At a few minutes to six, there was a knock on my door. She came into the room looking a lot happier than the day before.

"You find room?" I asked.

"Yes. Have room *Naklua* but cannot go until tomorrow. Ok I stay with you tonight?"

"Of course it is." I was happy for her but sorry for myself because it meant this would be our last night together.

"You no want take lady?"

"No. Have lady already – you!" I replied with mock anger. She laughed.

The evening went well. We had a great meal, walked hand-in-hand along Beach Road, watched a movie at Royal Garden, talked, joked, stopped for a nightcap and then strolled, arm-in-arm, back to the hotel. It was a different experience to any I had ever had in Pattaya. She was a bar girl, I knew that, but there was not a hint of bar-speak coming from her lips. We had slept together but had not had sex. And now, she was making me feel like I was seventeen again and we were out on our first date. I was happier than a pig in shit and in spite of my grandstanding that I was going to be a butterfly and not get involved, I didn't want it to end.

Back at the hotel, I showered and donned my shorts and t-shirt. She showered and again emerged fully dressed. This time though, when we got into bed, there was no space between us. We held each other closely and, as one thing led to another, we made love. Sex is what happens when two people get into bed together, naked, with full knowledge of the purpose of the exercise. Making love is what happens when two people, fully clothed, hold each other and allow the intimacy to evolve. We made love and when we woke in the morning, were no longer just good friends.

We had an early breakfast because she had to catch a bus to *Rayong* to collect the rest of her clothes. She was going to take them to her new apartment and we arranged to meet back at the hotel at 6:00pm. There was no hint of her actually staying in her apartment, at least while I was in Pattaya. We kissed goodbye and I spent the day counting down the hours until six o'clock.

When it arrived, she was on time as usual. She had completed her moving-in job without any problems and arrived at my door looking radiant. We decided to go to dinner and then watch a cabaret show. When I look back over my life, I can easily pinpoint pivotal events that changed its course. With the benefit of hindsight, I can look back and say, "If I could change that decision, my life today would be very different." My choice of going to watch a cabaret show was one such point in my life and if by some miracle I could turn back the clock, I would not have gone within a mile of the place. My life was about to become totally 'different'.

We took our seats at about ten o'clock, ordered drinks and were enjoying the show. It would not have been more than fifteen minutes later that I felt I was being stared at. I looked to the other side of our table to find none other than Blondie standing there with hands on hips, glaring at me. She rattled off something in Thai, which I did not understand. I replied, "I went to see you at your bar and you were not there. You go with other *fa-lung*. What can I do?" This was my standard response to an irate bar girl and although it was lies and guesswork, more often than not it turned out to be accurate.

My girlfriend was getting very uneasy.

"I no want problem with bar girl", she pleaded.

I tried to reassure her that everything was ok but she started to get up to leave. I asked her to sit down and told Blondie to go away. She sat and Blondie left. Now, with any brains at all, I would have suggested we leave immediately. My girlfriend clearly wanted to, but I truly did believe that was the end of the matter. We stayed to watch the show.

It was close to one o'clock when we both agreed to call it a night. I was looking forward to getting back to the hotel and making love with her again. I motioned the waiter that we wished to check bin. Then the strangest thing happened. It happened so fast that it was over before I realized what had actually occurred and tragically, before I had the chance to change the course of events that followed. I suddenly felt arms fold around me from behind and someone kissing me on the cheek and neck.

The next thing I saw was a hand come from behind me and toss a 1,000 *baht* note in front of my girlfriend. She got up to leave, crying, "I no want problem," while I was being kept firmly in my seat by the girl holding me from behind. Meanwhile, the 1,000 *baht* was being pushed to my girlfriend again. As I said, it was all over before I realized what had happened. My girlfriend ran off. I turned to see the face of the intruder. It was Blondie again. She was pleading, "I love you. I love you."

"What the fuck have you done?" I demanded as I handed her back the money my girlfriend had not taken.

"I love you. I love you," was all she would say.

My girlfriend was gone. Foolishly, I had not bothered to ask her the name of the apartment building where she was staying. I had no idea where it was, other than it was in *Naklua*. I was furious. After paying the bill, I walked out into the night with Blondie hot on my heels.

The epilogue to this story is that my card-playing LTTG#2 found herself another *fa-lung* and the last I heard was that she went to Denmark and was doing quite nicely thank you. This is in spite of her previous assurances that she would die without me.

I never saw my would-be girlfriend again although a handwritten note, in English, was left at my hotel thanking me sincerely for everything and wishing me well for the future. I still have the note and it is one of my most cherished possessions. As for me, I survived, but not a day goes by that I don't think about that night and what might have been.

And Blondie? Well, she let her hair grow, let it return to its natural black colour and promised never to have it curled again. As my LTTG#3, we lived together for the next eighteen months, meaning she beat the previous pair as far as relationship longevity goes.

So, what can I say? A famous Australian once lamented, "Such is life." I would be tempted to say the same thing except the expression has a very poor track record. Seconds after he uttered those immortal words, Edward (Ned) Kelly was hanged.

20

Up The Country

Against incredibly stiff competition, I have had to seize the crown and declare myself to be the most stupid *fa-lung* in Thailand. I was going to declare myself to be the stupidest man in Thailand but that would have put me up against Thai men and, as every foreigner here knows, in any contest between a *fa-lung* and a Thai, the *fa-lung* can never win.

I have recently returned from a four-day trip into the provinces to visit my latest batch of in-laws. The act of insanity was that I agreed to go in the first place. Having performed this onerous duty on three prior occasions, once with each of my three past loves, I knew exactly what to expect, should have known better, but went anyway. I had run out of excuses why I could not go and the masochist in me needed to be taken out for exercise.

I have already written about a trip to *Kam Phaeng Phet* to visit my first girlfriend's family, 'Relatively Speaking', but did not keep notes or write about trips two (*Korat*) and three (*Trat*) simply because they were much of the same - without the deer-hunting grandfather. I actually need to write about this last trip, not because it was anything special or exciting but because I need to vent my spleen and, more importantly, I need a written record to refer back to if I am tempted to repeat the experience in the future.

On this, trip number four, I will not mention the name of the town and will refer to my girlfriend as *Lek* - not her real name. This is for no other reason than self-preservation. If one of her English literate friends or some treacherous *fa-lung* relays the contents of this story back to her, I could wake up one morning with a meat-cleaver between my eyes.

A century ago, the great Australian journalist, balladist, short-story writer and poet, Henry Lawson, said it best in his poem, "Up The Country".

"I am back from up the country — very sorry that I went
Seeking for the Southern poets' land whereon to pitch my tent;
I have lost a lot of idols, which were broken on the track,
Burnt a lot of fancy verses, and I'm glad that I am back.
Further out may be the pleasant scenes of which our poets boast,
But I think the country's rather more inviting round the coast.
Anyway, I'll stay at present at a boarding house in town,
Drinking beer and lemon squashes, taking baths and cooling down."
'Up The Country' by Henry Lawson

Mr Lawson, of course, was writing about outback Australia but if you talk about Thailand, the story's the same thing. Like me, he preferred city life. I am a city slicker and I make no apologies for that. If I am living in a place where it takes me longer than ten minutes of traveling to obtain something I need or want, I move.

We got off the bus at *Morchit* Bus Terminal and I collected the sixty kilogram suitcase from the luggage compartment. We had already agreed (I was told) we would have something to eat at *Morchit*. My fleet-footed little sparrow hastened away with me in pursuit. Passing many small restaurants with *a-roi* smelling food, I wondered which one would pass her inspection.
"What is the rush?" I asked, "Don't you want to sit down and eat?"
"Buy ticket first. Eat after."

"Ok. You're the boss."
She found the ticket booth and bought two tickets. I asked how often the buses leave.

"All the time", was her reply.

"When does our bus leave?"
She scanned the tickets in her hand. "Now."
This was particularly disappointing for me because, for the first time in our relationship, I was actually hungrier than my little eating machine.

Three hours later, the world's slowest coach crawled into *Nakhon Nowhere*. It was while we were waiting for Papa to pick us up that *Lek* admitted she did not actually live in *Nakhon Nowhere*. She lived in that province but not actually in the big, convenient, comfortable city itself. She lived in *Nakhon Nowhere Noi*, some thirty-five kilometres away, and Papa would take us the rest of the journey.

Papa, Mama and *Lek's* young sister duly arrived per a well cared for Toyota pick-up. Pleasantries were exchanged and, with me in the front passenger seat, we headed off to *Nakhon Nowhere Noi*.

Once there, I found out she did not actually live in *Nakhon Nowhere Noi* proper, but some thirteen kilometres out of the small town. We continued the drive and, at about the thirteen kilometre mark, I noticed some nice houses along the side of the road. Papa turned off along a dirt road that I assumed was the driveway to one of them. As everything resembling a house disappeared in the rear-view mirror, the driveway turned into a collection of potholes some three kilometres long, at the very end of which was a nest of four or five dwellings set in the midst of a cane field.

The enclave was a true family affair. Uncles, aunts and grandparents all lived side by side in typical Thai fashion. *Lek's* home was two-storey, neat and tidy, built of wood with concrete stumps. *Lek* explained the dirt floor was only going to be temporary because, "Mama want make cement floor. Only 10,000 *baht*." Great. Upstairs was one large room in which all of us would be sleeping, side by side. Downstairs was a well-kept kitchen with newly-tiled floor plus a shower/toilet room.

The toilet was a European pedestal but flushing involved a bucket and plastic ladle. *Lek* apologized.

"Mama like to make *horng nahm soo-ay*. Maybe need 5,000 *baht*." That would be nice.

She then gave me a brief tour of the estate in which four mangy, flea-ridden dogs, one cat and a family of fighting chickens had free reign. My problem is that I would like to make dogs an endangered species by annihilating the vast majority of them, starting with these four. Tour completed, *Lek* then proceeded to help Mama prepare the evening meal while Papa and I discovered we shared a liking for *Beer Chang*.

We ate the meal on the wooden bench outside the kitchen and, as always, it was delicious. Why do Western women need eight hours to prepare a meal for two when Thais can cook up a banquet for five in ten minutes? Another of life's mysteries. *Lek's* parents appreciated that I ate everything placed before me. Little did they know how hungry I was after missing a crucial meal earlier in the day. By 8:30pm, we were all ready for bed. We took turns for a shower while Mama attempted to coerce the younger sister to sleep. Papa locked up downstairs, *Lek* unfurled the mosquito net over our bed and I fell asleep.

The next day, Friday, was designated for sightseeing. We jumped into daddy's car and set off on our adventure. *Lek* said we were going to some place *soo-ay*. Five hours later we had driven through some of the most boring countryside in Thailand. I regretted that I had not brought my passport with me because I was certain we must have been close to one of Thailand's borders. I was also getting extremely annoyed with myself for finding a girlfriend who lived at the geographic centre of a circle with a five-hour radius in which there was nothing of man-made or natural interest. Maybe in the mountainous north or the coastal south of Thailand the scenery is picturesque, but where we went, the landscape was totally devoid of anything to photograph or remember.

Lek occasionally interrupted the drudgery with poignant commentary. "You see house here?"

"Yes, I see."

"*Soo-ay mai?*"

"Yes. *Soo-ay.*"

"How much you think to buy same same?"

"I don't know."

"Maybe 100,000 *baht. Nakhon Nowhere* very cheap."

Oh goodie goodie.

Finally the stops for food became more frequent and I was convinced we were getting near our destination. Through the steam cloud emanating from my frustration and anger, the end to my torment appeared as a small mountain stream with a series of man-made waterfalls and picnic areas. At a guess, there were around five hundred people there happily swimming, eating and frolicking. We gathered together all the food and started walking towards the stream in search of a suitable picnic spot. The level, neatly-grassed and shaded area I selected was passed aside in favour of, some three hundred metres later, the ant-ridden, fly-infested, rock-studded precipice upon which we finally perched.

The mats laid out and the food set down, my girlfriend asked if I wanted to go swimming. Surveying the scene about me, I came to the conclusion that, with so many people eating, drinking and frolicking in the water and the toilet block some five hundred metres away, the yellowish colour of the water was probably due to urine and not mud churned up by the swift-flowing falls. Do I really want dysentery? The true decision maker was watching, upstream, a young lad disgorging the contents of his stomach into the water. "No thank you."

The scene of so many people enjoying themselves with simple pleasures was joyous to watch but the pointed rock beneath my sensitive backside was unforgiving. Sitting cross-legged is not a comfortable experience for *fa-lung* either and I soon found out that, no matter how I positioned my legs, something was digging into some part of my anatomy and the blood circulation was being deprived from another.

As much as I wanted to enjoy myself, it was difficult. All I could think about was the five-hour trip back to the house. They must have noticed my disappointment and Mama apologized that the stream was not as *soo-ay* as usual because there had been no rain for some time. I truthfully replied that it was not a problem.

D⌐y three began quietly as I stayed in bed for as long as I could get away with it. Once I was finally forced to get up, *Lek* asked what I wanted to do today. Foolishly I did not scream out "Go back to Pattaya!" My silence brought about two options. We could all go to a Korean restaurant for a barbecue lunch or we could buy some fish and cook it here. My consideration was not whether I wanted to eat pork or fish but purely financial. I knew I would be paying so the restaurant idea sounded too expensive. Better to buy fish from the market.

We all piled into the car for the trip. I don't know what brought it on but *Lek* mentioned the fish market was very close to the place we had been on the previous day. No-o-o-o-o-o-o-o-o! Not another five-hour drive just to buy some bloody fish! Please, I've changed my mind – I want Korean!
"Why are you crying?" she asked.
"Sore eyes," I lied.
Where is a McDonalds when you want one? I would have happily shouted Filet-o-fish burgers for everyone but, just like policemen, there is never one around when you need one.

Lek kept me entertained by pointing out some local places of interest along the way.
"Mama want house here. On big road. Easy to get taxi. You think good or not?"
"Good idea."
"Not much money for buy land."
Thank you for sharing that with me.

Sitting silently in the front passenger seat, I glanced at the fuel guage and noticed the indicator was just above 'E'. Papa appeared unconcerned so he must have been one of those 'when it reads 'E' there is still ten litres left in the tank' kind of guys. I counted the number of petrol stations we passed as the indicator gradually nudged 'E'. Nine and a half litres later, we arrived at the small open-air fish market which seemed to be housing twice as many customers as it was fish.

Mama and *Lek* threw themselves into the fray. One half-hour of sniffing, poking, prodding and three medium-sized fish were purchased and brought to the car.
"You're fucking kidding!" I wanted to scream.
"All this way for three stinking fish? If I drove this far, I'd want to buy a container load of the bastards!"
But I kept my mouth shut.

During the return trip we passed two petrol stations that Papa again ignored. I took the initiative and handed five hundred *baht* to *Lek* telling her to explain to Papa that this was for fuel. I could take it no more.

Before continuing, I must speak about *Lek's* younger sister. Many times, when the *fa-lung* is introduced to his girlfriend's younger sibling, it is really her own child. This time, in spite of the large age gap between them, I was convinced they were telling the truth. She looked nothing like *Lek*.

The younger sister was just over two years old and extremely fat. Now I knew why - she never stopped eating. Every time she opened her mouth, food was shoved in it. And she never stopped opening her mouth. I wanted to explain that fat children grow into fat adults and their lives are made hell but I did not want to interfere. The fastest way to lose the interest of Thais is to tell them what to do.

On one occasion I watched the brat playing with two puppies belonging to one of the neighbours. Even though I don't like dogs, I can not abide cruelty to animals. She picked up one of the puppies, its eyes barely open, grabbing it by the head then shaking it by the legs all to the laughter of the family. Only two of us were not amused – me and the puppy. I was relieved when Mama took the puppy away from the brat but my joy was short-lived. She simply held the thing by its front paws and forced it to dance on her lap. She was showing the brat how to truly torture an animal.

This child was given everything and anything it wanted. She was indulged, petted, pampered and feted with her every whim treated as a demand by an eager and obliging Mama, Papa and sister. She was allowed to eat anything, destroy anything, waste anything and kill anything and never chastised, smacked or told "no". Teaching her right from wrong did not seem to be a priority and she was the most spoiled little brat I have ever met.

I would like child psychologists to come here and undertake a study of spoiled children to determine just how many of them turn out to be violent adults or serial killers. I was raised in the old school of the 'a child should be seen and not heard' and 'spare the rod and spoil the child' doctrines. Whenever I got out of line, a clip behind the ear usually brought me back to earth.

If my parents were right (and so far, I have not killed a packet of Cornflakes or Coco Pops), then in fifteen or so years time, all of Thailand will be shocked by the news of an extremely fat and disturbed female student taking an AK47 and cutting a swathe through her classmates because they stole the ten donuts she had brought for her pre-lunch snack. They will hear my cry of "I told you so" clear in South America.

At one point *Lek* asked if the brat could come and stay with us in Pattaya for a week to give Mama a rest. I am going to buy the most comprehensive English-Thai dictionary on the market because the phrase, "When hell freezes over," does not appear in my current one. She did however get the message from the daggers in my eyes and the steam coming out of my ears. Words became superfluous.

Sunday morning, I was rudely awakened by the sound of *Lek* screaming "*gin kao.*" As a lazy *fa-lung* I was the last one out of bed and hobbled down the stairs for my morning wake-up cup of coffee and nicotine ingestion. *Lek* asked what I wanted to do today. They had nothing planned so it was up to me. I mentioned I was still tired from all the traveling and excitement, so I would prefer to stay around the house. Not a problem. I had a shower, ate breakfast and the day was spent watching Thai TV shows.

Monday was the Mother's Day public holiday in Thailand. On this day gifts of respect are given to Mothers in strict order of age. Daughters give to their mothers and younger mothers give to older ones. Apart from the brat, my darling was the youngest in the pecking order and her mother was the youngest of four sisters. This meant she (i.e. me) gave gifts to Mama, Mama's three sisters and grandmother. Mama, of course, had no money. This meant that Mama had to be given extra money for gifts for her three elder sisters and her mother. Quick addition revealed I paid out for nine Mother's day gifts in total. What a good man. Thankfully, Mama's sisters did not know I was coming otherwise it could have been fifteen! Grandmother, of course, was ecstatic. Being at the top of the gift pyramid, she scored big time.

Later in the day I was told we were going to see something big in *Nakhon Nowhere* city. I was hoping it was not another ruined temple. I've seen enough temples, ruined or otherwise, to last me a lifetime and if I had to see another one I'd scream.

What a shock that the first stop was at an ATM. My strategy had been to tell *Lek* that I did not bring much money with me because I was saving up for something really important. I thought this would pre-empt the exorbitant financial demands that would certainly arise. After the earlier gift-giving spree, I had about 1,000 baht in cash left to get us back to Pattaya. Unfortunately she was smarter than I thought and could possibly smell the ATM card I had secreted on my person. I was pushed out the door with a "make sure you get enough for everybody this time, you cheap Charlie!" look on her face. What could I do? I was trapped.

Back into the car full of much happier people, it was not long before we stopped at the big attraction.
"A-a-a-a-a-a-a-h!"
My scream frightened the relatives somewhat but I passed it off that some insect had bitten me. I walked around the big old ruined temple with family in tow making sure the ATM card and the fresh crisp 1,000 *baht* notes did not get too far out of their sight. Twenty minutes and ten photos later, we were done.

Tuesday morning arrived not quickly enough. Surprisingly, I was the first to get up. I had showered and packed away my toothbrush and razor before anyone noticed I was awake. *Lek* stirred and asked if I wanted coffee just as I was carrying the suitcase down the stairs.

I did not eat any breakfast explaining that I had a bit of an upset stomach. My urgency did not rub off and it was not until 11:00am that we were all ready for the trip into *Nakhon Nowhere*.

Saying goodbye is always an emotional experience so I sat on the bus and waited for *Lek* to get it over with. She eventually joined me and tearfully sipped on her bottle of water as the bus pulled out of the station and I fell asleep.

Once at *Morchit*, I took charge. My impatience had waned and we sat to eat a meal *before* buying the tickets to Pattaya. That final leg was the easiest of all and again, I slept most of the way.

Try as I might, I could not contain my joy at being back home in my apartment in my city of Pattaya, where the last few lines of Henry Lawson's poem repeated in my head.

"I intend to stay at present,
As I said before, in town,
Drinking beer and lemon-squashes,
Taking baths and cooling down."

21

The Bluebird of Happiness

They say it happens to every male from time to time so not to worry about it. Very common and nothing to be ashamed of. It is all very well to say that, but when it happens to you, no amount of conciliatory comments can negate the all pervasive feeling that this is the beginning of the end, that dysfunctional sex is going to be the norm from now on and eventually the desire for sex will decrease to match the level of non-performance. Yes, I'm talking about impot... (I can't even write the word!) Let's call it 'brewer's droop'.

It happened on one of my earlier trips to Pattaya. Of all the places on earth for it to happen, this has got to be the worst. Why couldn't it have happened when I was visiting 17th century monasteries in France or on one of the 'Over thirty's' nights I reluctantly attended at my local football club back in Australia? Why not when I was watching a group of bare-breasted tribal women from New Guinea perform a rain dance on National Geographic? That would have been a blessing. But no, true to Murphy's Law, it had to happen in the fun capital of Asia, possibly the world.

On this particular trip I was 'between girlfriends' which meant I was planning to join the 'butterfly' ranks and hover between conquests until I found the next Miss Right. There were no constraints or limitations on what was to be two weeks spent randomly sampling Pattaya's delights.

As is usually the case, the best laid plans of mice, men and me come unstuck. My first night in Pattaya was spent catching up with old friends - many old friends. I have no idea when the night finished, but I was incapable of walking let alone initiating a mating ritual with a Thai hostess. The second night was mostly spent fulfilling appointments that I could vaguely recall making the night before. Result – tired, emotional and forced to use gutter-to-gutter navigational techniques to crawl back to my hotel room alone. Next night – strike three. There came a point in the evening when I could see the beautiful women about me and I knew I wanted them but could not remember why.

The following morning I came to the hangover-inspired conclusion that the partying had to stop and I needed to return my focus to the whole point of the trip. I reasoned it was possible to drink myself into a coma anywhere I traveled in the world but it was not possible to get laid with as little effort as it takes in Pattaya. Therefore the alcohol abuse must stop or at least be limited to socially acceptable levels.

That evening I avoided my friends so I would not be coerced into the many rounds of drinks that always accompany inane conversation. My concentration was securely focused on the lovely hostess who served me my orange juice. A bit of quick banter and I made my decision. She was beautiful and smiling and gleefully accepted my offer of a night away from her arduous bar work. We left the bar together and headed for a quick bite to eat before retiring to the comfort and sanctuary of my hotel room.

We showered together and, with my desire heightened by three consecutive nights of celibacy, retired to the bed. This is when the rot set in. No matter how beautiful and willing she was and no matter what she did, the message did not get through to that most important part of my anatomy. He was asleep and determined to stay that way. Anger, frustration, confusion and disappointment swelled my senses, eventually leading to the one emotion that is the final nail in the coffin for any desired sexual activity – worry. The more you worry about it, the worse it gets. The lady blamed herself but I knew that was not the case. I passed it off as being tired and said we would try again in the morning.

I was hoping this was in fact the case but it still took a long time before I finally fell asleep.

Next morning I awoke to find 'my son me' in a partially conscious condition. This was a good start and I believed that with some encouragement, he could be woken to the satisfaction of all parties. My companion also noticed his semi-active state and began providing a little encouragement. Alas, he went back to sleep. Along with worry, I could now add severe embarrassment to my pool of emotions. I cut the morning short, made some pitiful excuses to my companion and ushered her out the door with double the usual amount I provide for overnight encounters. My hope was she would recognize the extra cash as 'hush money' and not spread it around her bar that this particular *fa-lung* was a total dud. Leaving nothing to chance, I decided never to return to her bar.

Sitting in my hotel room staring at my hitherto useful appendage was the loneliest I have ever felt in my life. My best friend was becoming my worst enemy and he had let me down in the most catastrophic way. Thankfully, before reaching the conclusion that my life was effectively over, I reasoned my non-performance the night before was probably due to the severe alcohol hammering to which I had subjected my body. My non-performance that morning was probably due to excessive worry about the night before. What was needed was a successful performance to restore my confidence and remove any self-doubt. But how?

The enforcement of Thailand's pharmaceutical laws being somewhat ineffectual, I recalled that Viagra can be purchased over the counter at some pharmacies. I had read a little about Viagra in the press but until now, had never felt the need. At this point I would have tried anything, so Viagra was definitely worth a shot.

Feeling like the schoolboy purchasing his first pack of condoms, I loitered outside the pharmacy and waited until the other customers left. Discretely peering throught the glass door, I noticed that, true to form, the only attendant was a young female. It did not matter because, once the last customer finally departed, it was time to bite the bullet. After all, I had waited twenty minutes for the opportunity. Nothin's gonna stop me now.

"Do you sell Viagra?" I asked sheepishly.

"Sell one - 500 *baht*," was her expressionless reply.

Except that.

"Ok. I'll have one please." It was too late for financial concerns. Just then, some English-speaking tourists entered the shop and I changed colour to bright red as I noticed them watching the pharmacist cut one little blue tablet from the easily recognizable blister-pack of four.

"You want instructions?" she asked rather loudly.

"Yes," I whispered.

The only more embarrassing situation would be if I was buying haemorrhoid suppositories and John Cleese was the pharmacist. I handed over the money and left the shop via the keyhole.

Back in the sanctuary of my room, I opened the instruction pamphlet and read like a man possessed. I was disturbed to learn of the possible side effects and the dangers. Since I had never had any heart or respiratory problems in the past, I decided any other possible side effects were worth the risk. I was happy to read that the effects of Viagra were not dramatically reduced by the consumption of alcohol, drinking coffee or smoking cigarettes. Unfortunately I have all three vices. Still, the 100mg tablet looked a bit drastic for a first attempt. I used a sharp knife to cut the little blue pill into four pieces. I would try 25mg first and, if that did not work, would try 50mg the next time.

That night I ventured to a different bar area in search of a guinea pig on whom I could test the narcotic solution to my problem. It took only two bars and four orange juices to find a likely candidate. I remembered reading that Viagra should be taken about one hour before the expected sexual activity, so at about 11:00pm I went to the toilet. Alone, I crunched and swallowed the one-quarter piece I had secreted in a small plastic bag in my pocket. My plan was to be back in the room with a playmate by midnight.

Sitting back at the bar, I was happily chatting with my newly found love when I detected motion in my groin area. Shuffling in the seat made the movement more intense and, since this was not a normal situation for me, I deduced the Viagra was starting to take effect. It had only been fifteen minutes. Check bin!

The walk to the *baht* bus and then from the road outside my hotel to the room proved a little too much for my-son-me. He started to test his might against the denim of my jeans, having already slithered beneath the elastic of my underpants. Once in the room I made a run for the shower and there, in private, undressed to take a good look at the monster I had created. My first thought was one of sadness, since it was apparent the Viagra had neither made my best friend longer nor thicker as I had hoped. Life is full of disappointments. But, it was solid! I felt like I could lift dumbbells with it. Any more blood flowed in there and it would surely explode. When my lady joined me in the shower, she was visibly impressed.

I can report that the night's performance was back to my usual standard of mediocrity. In fact, it exceeded mediocre by the mere duration of the act. This time, instead of having to mentally picture my grandmother playing football for Liverpool in order to stave off premature orgasm, I found myself fantasizing about an orgy involving me and twenty or so Hollywood bimbettes in order to bring it on.

Finally, spent and exhausted, I lay beside my smiling lady and waited for my appendage to lose its enthusiasm. A great weight had been lifted from my mind and a load of worries released from my body. In the morning, I woke up second. My-son-me had already stirred and was standing at attention to salute the new day. Round two was just as good as the earlier bout.

According to the instruction leaflet, the effects were supposed to last around eight hours. Walking along Beach Road some sixteen hours after my ingestion of the quarter tablet, I can state that, for me at least, the effects still had not worn off. It seemed you-know-who was reacting to any form of friction or stimulation. Even the following evening, some twenty-four hours later, I was not unhappy it was still going on. Another night of passion and my confidence and libido were fully

"... his bloody viagra is killing me!"

restored. The true test would be the third night when surely the effects would have worn off. It would be then that the Gods would determine whether my sex life was back to normal or whether I could look forward to a life of chemical dependence.

To my great relief, the drug-free night went well. Since then, I still resort to the little blue helpers when the occasion arises, or should I say, doesn't arise. It is my backup plan for the times when having a few quiet beers with my friends turns into a marathon session of swapping war stories, tales of sexual prowess and other lies.

WARNING
Do not consume Viagra without first consulting a medical practitioner.

22

Snow Job

Once upon a time in The Land of Lies, lived a poor family of Mama, Papa and their beautiful daughter, Snow Job. Like many people living in The Land of Lies, they had aspirations to be rich but did not really want to work for the money. It happened that Mama had a very clever and very wealthy sister, Mama San, who observed their plight and decided to come to her sister's aid.

"I am opening a new tavern in Fun Town and I want Snow Job to come and work for me," she said. "Many foreigners with big money come to Fun Town and it will be easy for Snow Job to get a lot of money for you."

"But Snow Job has been kept pure and innocent all this time in readiness to marry a young, rich and handsome man from The Land of Lies. I don't want her to be defiled by a foreign devil, or worse, to marry one," Mama pleaded.

"She doesn't have to," Mama San assured her. "She does not have to give herself to the foreign dogs. She merely has to be her beautiful charming self and give the illusion she is available for marriage. I will have her protected at all times. The money will start rolling in, you'll see."

Mama reluctantly agreed with her cunning sister. After all, she was much smarter and richer and seemed to have all the answers. Thus the

126

plan was born and Snow Job, under the charge of Mama San, moved to Fun Town. Mama San arranged for her most trusted and ugliest servant, Pegasus, to be Snow Job's guardian and protector. She would pretend to be Snow Job's best friend and remain at her side constantly so as to quickly expunge any foreigner who tried to get too close to the bait.

The idea was very simple. Snow Job would work as a waitress in the tavern and be her beautiful, charming self. The men would be attracted but always kept at a safe distance. The bait would be dangled before them until they were caught hook, line and sinker. Then she would be offered to the love-struck victim, but only after he had paid a 'bride fee'. This was standard practice in The Land of Lies. Once the money was handed over, Snow Job would suddenly lose interest in her paramour and exit the scene until such time as he gave up the chase. The phony wedding would be called off, the victim would return home and Snow Job could begin work on the next pigeon.

And it came to pass that, in no time at all, into this neatly packaged net of deception stumbled Sir Gullible. Aloft a donkey possessing more brains than he did, Sir Gullible was neither a Knight nor of Noble birth. He was a simple low-life who found a wandering donkey, mounted it, was arrested for bestiality but eventually released when the donkey refused to testify. He then decided - Sir Gullible not the donkey - to seek adventure in the Land of Lies.

From the moment he first saw Snow Job, our hero was besotted and he fell for every line as easily as falling off a log. His attentions to Snow Job did not go unnoticed and the plan went like clockwork. She played the game, Mama San watched and waited while Pagasus kept guard. As soon as Mama San was certain he was past the point of no return, she swung into action.

Snow Job told him Mama and Papa were coming to Fun Town to meet him. He was nervous because her mother could not speak a word of his native language and thus the communication gap was wider than the Grand Canyon. When he arrived at the tavern on the appointed night, he was told Mama wanted to speak with him alone. Even though he understood almost none of her conversation, he did understand when she asked him if he really loved Snow Job. He replied in the affirmative after which, Mama got down to the nitty gritty and a figure of 100,000 gold pieces was mentioned as the bride fee for her daughter.

It was rather expensive by local standards as most foreigners were asked for less than half this amount. But the words 'virgin' were mentioned so as to justify the excessive fee. Sir Gullible simply kept nodding and agreeing. It wasn't until the matter of urgency raised its head that alarm bells started ringing. Next week, ok? Sure, no problem. He was so controlled by the proceedings that he failed to mention to Mama that he was in the middle of a cash-flow crisis and thus some 99,900 gold pieces short of the agreed figure.

He was finally given a reprieve from the one-sided conversation when Mama San, who spoke a little of his language, joined them. After a brief chat between the two ladies, Mama San told him the figure of 100,000 was excessive (a point of agreement) and that she had reduced it to 80,000 for him. She then went on to say that once he married Snow Job, she would let him have one of the many houses she owned in the capital city of The Land of Lies. The 'let him have' statement was vague enough to allow a presumption of magnanimous generosity on the part of Mama San.

She followed this with the observation that next month, between the 1st and the 15th, was an auspicious time for a marriage. Again with the urgency. Further, she would pay for the wedding and asked how many of his friends he would like to invite along. Next came an offer to buy Snow Job a gold chain, bracelet and ring for the occasion. The pot was being sweetened.

With the bait taken, a figure of 80,000 gold pieces agreed upon and a timeframe imposed, the trap was ready to be sprung. Their idea was that he should hand over the loot immediately so they could pretend to be making the wedding plans. Snow Job could then play her part by becoming cold and evasive to her paramour. With the help of the ever present Pegasus, who would make life as difficult as possible for him,

128

it was hoped he would soon lose interest and disappear back to wherever he came from.

Once the two ladies left, Sir Gullible ordered a tankard of ale and settled down to ponder his next move. Running away came immediately to mind and did appear to be his best option, but the lure of Snow Job was too strong. He wanted to have his cake and eat it too.

It is said the Gods protect fools and children. Luckily for the middle-aged Sir Gullible, he fell under this heavenly umbrella. Unbeknown to the two conspirators, he was not what he appeared to be. He may have given the illusion of wealth but in fact, was as poor as a church mouse. Their greedy little clutches would never see any of his money because, basically, he had none. He had already confessed this sad fact to Snow Job but she had failed to pass on the critical information to the puppeteers.

When they eventually found out a few days later, they were both shocked at the unforeseen spanner in the works. Mama was furious and her first instinct was to snatch Snow Job back to their home and forget all about any more 'get rich quick' schemes. Mama San, on the other hand, blamed herself for not being able to detect a penniless scoundrel sooner.

There was another problem. Because of her youth and inexperience, Snow Job actually felt something for Sir Gullible. What began as simply feeling sorry for her hapless victim turned into a form of caring. She did not want to return to her village but, for richer or poorer, wanted to stay with our hero.

Back at their home, Mama and Papa were shaken by Snow Job's refusal to return. After some long telephone argument, Mama San settled things by saying that Snow Job could stay working at the tavern where she would be looked after. Sir Gullible, on the other hand, would be 'taken care of'. What she meant by that is anyone's guess, but she immediately went into a huddle with the menacing Pegasus to outline a strategy.

While this was going on, other plans were also being hatched. Snow Job informed Sir Gullible that Mama San was going to 'take care of him' and, for once in his miserable life, he took the hint. He never returned to the tavern again.

One afternoon, some days later, Mama San noticed Snow Job had not clocked in. Phone calls were made and a burly bodyguard sent to look for her. Her meagre possessions were not in her room and her cell phone remained unanswered. She had disappeared and their frantic search proved fruitless. Just before sunset, Mama received a phone call from her errant daughter and was informed of the unthinkable.

And, as the sun sank slowly in the East, off rode the happy Sir Gullible, aloft a donkey still possessing more brains than he did, with his lovely Snow Job walking dutifully along side. It would be poignant to end this fantasy by saying "and they lived happily ever after", but with no money, no prospects and only 'love' to see them through, what do you think?

23

From the Front Lines

The background to this story is that I wrote a book called *Money Number One*, which is a light-hearted guide for male visitors to Pattaya. I mention this for two reasons. Firstly, it is a great opportunity to give my book a free plug and secondly, the book contained a vital message for my fellow *fa-lung*. I advised those men with a Thai girlfriend to never buy her a mobile phone. I argued that the mobile phone may be convenient and a great way to keep in touch but, in my opinion, it is a girl's greatest weapon. I guarantee, at some point of the relationship, it will be used to your disadvantage.

In the very beginning of our relationship, I disclosed my views on mobile phones to my girlfriend, *Pom*. I explained that I did not like using mobile phones and concluded with the statement that I was never going to buy one for myself, let alone her. There was tacit, if not reluctant, acceptance.

Two weeks later, her mother paid us a visit here in Pattaya. Thankfully it was only for the day but, when she left, I found out the visit had a specific purpose. She left a gift for her daughter – a mobile phone. The excuse was that she missed her very much and wanted to be able to talk with her whenever she needed to. I was unimpressed but what could I do? It was fait accompli. My little darling was very pleased and took to the advanced technology like a duck to water. She knew how to program it, play games on it and store ten thousand telephone numbers on it. I learned how to switch it off.

Over the next few months, the mobile phone was my lady's constant companion. She groomed it, doted over it and purchased a 'more *soo-ay*' cover for it. She even gave out the number to a few of my friend's girlfriends in a blatant attempt to make me see the advantages of joining the 21st century. I stubbornly refused to make a call, preferring to use a phonecard at the local phone booth on the very rare occasions I needed to call someone.

I did discover something very disturbing though. Thais have no conception of etiquette when it comes to calling someone on the telephone. Personally, unless prior arrangements were made, I would never entertain the thought of calling someone before noon or after nine o'clock at night. Admittedly, this is because most of my friends are incoherent after 9:00pm and usually sleeping off hangovers every morning. My sweetheart, on the other hand, made and received calls at all hours of the day and night. Mama call at 3:00am? *Mai mee bun hah.*

It was some weeks later that *Pom* went home to her village for three days. Immediately upon her return, I was met with an overload of TLC. Then it began.
"You not angry me *na*?"
Every instinct told me not to pursue this conversation, but I could not help myself. Ok, I'll bite.
"Why?"
"I not know what happen. I change bus at *Morchit* but when get off bus, I no have telephone. I think somebody *kamoyee* [stole] telephone me."
Is that all?
"I'm not angry. It was your phone, not mine."
"But we need telephone."
I noted the use of the royal 'we' in that sentence.
"No. I don't need a telephone. I told you I hate telephones," came my reply.

"But Mama buy for me new telephone."

She ratted through her bag and produced a box containing a new mobile phone. She then showed me the receipt for six thousand *baht*. I was not sure where all this was leading but was soon to find out.

"Mama not have money so she borrow from brother she."

Still none of my business.

"You can help me please?"

The penny was slipping from my hand when – "She have to give brother back before end of month. You can give me please?" – and then it dropped.

"Why do I have to pay?"

"I have no money. Mama have no money and brother she need money back for pay rent."

There it was, in a nutshell. Whether the original mobile phone was really stolen at *Morchit* Bus Terminal or not, I did not know. Nor did it matter. Her mother had kindly given *Pom* a brand new replacement, bought with money she borrowed from her own brother. And who was ultimately responsible for the debt? Muggins. If I refused to pay, my *tee-ruk* would lose face. This would transfer to her mother who would lose considerable face at being unable to repay her brother. He, of course, would lose his entire head once he was evicted from his dwelling and forced to live under a coconut tree. I would be ultimately responsible for a whole village of faceless Thais and the guilt would be unbearable.

So, the overriding vital message for my fellow *fa-lung* is this - you cannot win. Simple as that. In spite of all my strongly-held convictions, I was merely play dough in the hands of a simple Thai girl. My mobile phone saga was just another skirmish in the battle of wits and I had come second. The Field Commander of the foreign forces noted that "the fight was lost but casualties were light," in his daily report from the front lines.

24

Water Water Everywhere

Thai people have an affinity for water. As proof of this, you only
need to wait until it rains. As soon as the first raindrops fall to
earth, instead of scurrying for shelter as most of us do, they don't
appear to worry too much. They will hurry to protect their goods and
chattels but, for themselves, take their time about seeking protection.
They will stand in the rain, walk in the rain and ride motorcycles through
the rain. Getting soaked to the skin does not appear to bother them and
walking around all day in dripping wet clothing is neither here nor there.
Do it for a week? Ah, *sanook sanook*. Bring on *Songkran*!

It is now the morning of April 20, 2002, and I have endured and
survived yet another *Songkran* festival. The festivities run from the
12th to the 19th of April - seven days of absolute mayhem that grip
Pattaya to wash away the sins of the previous year with the promise of
a fresh and prosperous beginning. At least, that is the theory. In my
opinion there is not enough water in the Gulf of Thailand to wash away
all Pattaya's sins of the previous year, but I digress.

Although much has already been written about it, for those of you
who don't know, the Thai New Year festival or *Songkran*, involves
water – lots of it. Traditionally it involved a small bowl of water and,
after seeking the other person's permission, sprinkling a few drops over
his hands or head and wishing him a happy new year. This gentle

ceremony has of course gone the way of the dinosaur with the modern day Pattaya version bearing no resemblance to its precursor.

I suppose it is like everything, really. Your doctor tells you a glass of red wine per day is good for your health. Obviously then, ten glasses of red wine a day must be really great for your health. If dabbing someone on the head with a few drops of water is good luck for them, then pouring a bucket of water over them and drenching them from head to foot must be exceptionally good luck for them.

Like many people, I used to blame foreigners for the *Songkran* excesses and believed that we were the ones responsible for taking a gentle and solemn Thai ceremony and turning it into a circus. Then I read an article by *Bangkok Post* columnist, Bernard Trink, which suggested this was an urban myth. The inference was that the Thais needed very little or no encouragement in the water festival transformation. The small bowl of water ritual just was not *sanook* enough.

As proof of this, witness the last and most voracious day of the games, the 19th. It begins early in the morning, before seven o'clock. Most *fa-lung* in Pattaya do not get out of bed until after midday so it is an all-Thai affair. Even late in the afternoon the players are almost exclusively Thai. Beach Road and Second Road are awash with water, powder and that white plaster emulsion used to make the victim resemble Casper the ghost. Both roads are transformed into one long parking lot as cars, trucks, motorbikes, *baht* taxis and pick-ups present themselves as targets for the pedestrian attackers. Pick-ups loaded with people and barrels of water return the fire with equal gusto.

The expats I know dislike *Songkran*. Every year, those with any money and Pattaya residents with brains take the opportunity to leave for a week's holiday. Most foreign bar owners hate *Songkran*. They would love to close their bars to prevent water damage. The authorities predicted that some 400,000 visitors would descend on Pattaya over the period. I would suggest that all except for a hundred or so of these would be Thais escaping Bangkok to participate in the fun at the beach.

In 2001, there were 554 deaths and 34,000 injuries over the New Year period. Most of these road accidents were blamed on a combination of alcohol and the throwing of water. Around eighty percent of the accidents involved motorcycles and it is easy to see why. No Western country would allow such madness for even one day, let alone seven. Certainly no Western country would tolerate the carnage attributed to the celebration. Imagine a January 1st free-for-all in Sydney, London or New York. Apart from the fact you would not need ice in the water in London or New York, since it would probably be snowing anyway, it would be a lawyer's dream and a policeman's nightmare.

I don't know about Europe or America but in Australia, shooting someone with a water pistol is classed as assault. Blasting them with a sustained burst of ice-cold water from a bazooka could be considered aggravated assault. Next we have wilful damage to public property, wilful damage to private property, causing a public nuisance, reckless endangerment, consuming alcohol in a public place, drunk and disorderly, sexual harassment, jaywalking, littering and the list goes on. This is not to mention the myriad of traffic violations, but since these are daily occurrences in Pattaya, not just over *Songkran*, I will not list all of the infringements here.

In 2002, in order to curb the mayhem, the *Pattaya Mail* reported, "Pattaya police issued a strong warning to all residents and tourists celebrating the *Songkran* festival that anyone found using ice, dangerous items like home-made water guns from PVC pipes, dirty water, or powder of any kind will be fined 2,000 *baht*. The warning stated that drunk and disorderly behaviour and any form of sexual harassment will also face strong penalties and a hefty fine. Police ask that everyone respect the traditional values of *Songkran* and Thai culture."

This was a waste of time, a waste of breath and a waste of ink. Politicians may grandstand about the horrific cost to the Nation of the water-throwing and powder-painting but they will not solve the problem by wishy-washy unenforceable laws about the size of the cannon or the water temperature. Out and about yesterday I saw thousands of the high-pressure water cannons, was hit by thousands of streams of ice water, was plastered white with powder from head to foot and did not see one policeman. As the only day of the festival where it is permissible to drench a policeman, something the Thai population is fully aware of, I can imagine pulling traffic duty on the 19th is not every police officer's ideal.

At a bar in *soi 8*, I was *len*ning *nahm* with the best and rest of them. Across the road a young child of four or five was also getting amongst it. Because he was so small, getting a better shot at his intended victim meant he had to get onto the road. Typically, he did not look before stepping out onto the street and twice a motorcyclist had to swerve to miss him. It did not take a genius to realize the danger this child was putting himself and others in. A motorcyclist only had to be blinded by a jet of water in the face at the same time the child stepped out and there may be a tragedy. Even if he did see the child in time he could lose control of the bike and injure himself, his three or four pillion passengers or some unfortunate bystander.

I expressed my concern to my Thai friend that this kid was about to become a statistic. She took a moment and then replied that all was ok because his mother and father were there. Obviously they were delinquent in their parental responsibilities but at least they were there to remove the body from the road after the tragedy. I moved to another location.

One way to stop the carnage would be to ban the practice altogether. Naturally enough, any politician who tried to do this in the Land of *Sanook* would be as popular as a fart in a spacesuit. Thai politicians are notorious for their shortcomings in the testicle department. But putting it in perspective, cigarette smoking and alcohol consumption kill more people annually and I don't see anyone, in any country, rushing out to ban either of those practices.

The way to survive *Songkran* is to have a strong sense of humour, a strong tolerance for water and be prepared. Take extra care on the streets. Do not plan on catching *baht* taxis anywhere. It is faster to walk. Go out only when necessary and when you do go out, dress in only light, casual, quick drying clothing. Expect to get totally soaking, dripping wet so when you are hit with water, don't get upset or angry. Don't wear a wristwatch unless it is waterproof to sixty metres. Better still, don't wear a watch. Similarly leave the mobile phone and camera at home. Put your cash into a re-sealable watertight plastic bag and, if you are a smoker, do the same with your cigarettes and lighter. Anything else you desperately need to take with you, keep in plastic bags. I use several plastic bags as the water always seems to penetrate the first one.

Another interesting article appeared in the *Bangkok Post* declaring, "Police have been banned from using water guns to shoot at passers-by during the *Songkran* celebration." It was reported that the Police Chief was concerned they might get confused and use their real firearms by mistake. It is extremely worrying to think Thai police do not have the capacity to differentiate between a large, pink, plastic, Star Wars type water pistol and their own small, heavy, metallic side-arm. This is good news for the criminals and Thai Mafia members who can be seen this morning collecting all of the discarded water pistols around town. And I thought they were merely out performing a public service!

25

Good News Week

A ll too often newspapers seem content to only bring tales of misfortune to their reader's attention. Sometimes these tales are tragic in their consequences. Most stories retold by foreigners in Thailand are merely anecdotal incidents that centre on miscommunication, misdirection and misunderstanding. They are benign enough and simply involve the foreigner paying out more money than he should have. Whether written in a newspaper or retold in a bar, 'feel good' stories are as rare as Thai lip-readers so, when I get the chance to relate one, I snap it up.

Occasionally, I go to Bangkok to visit a friend. His home is off Sukhumvit Road and since I don't have my own transportation, getting there involves a bus to Ekamai, crossing Sukhumvit, walking about one block then catching a *tuk-tuk* to his home. I tried walking once but it turned out to be much further than I expected and finding my way through the small *sois* that run off the *sois* that run off Sukhumvit was like navigating through a maze. Each one looked the same and I could never figure out the numbering system.

Signs are confusing as well. One signpost had an arrow pointing left saying 'Sukhumvit" and another arrow below it pointing right saying "Sukhumvit". Well, which was it? If I followed the left arrow would it mean I had to circumnavigate the earth before getting to Sukhumvit?

What I am trying to say is that I got lost. So now, when I visit, I show my friend's business card to a *tuk-tuk* driver and let him sort it out. The fare is a set thirty *baht* for everyone. It is not the case of *falung* paying thirty *baht* and Thais paying fifteen so, as such, I think it is reasonable.

The last time I visited, I ended up staying longer than anticipated and it was well after 9:00pm when I left his home. I needed to get to Ekamai to catch one of the last buses to Pattaya. As luck would have it, it was raining. Not heavy rain, just annoying drizzle. It is a very eerie feeling walking along deserted narrow streets late at night in the rain and I was praying for a *tuk-tuk* or any vehicle to appear so I did not feel so alone. I started walking in the direction of Sukhumvit.

Five minutes later my prayers were answered and a *tuk-tuk* approached me from behind. I hailed him down and said I wanted to get to Sukhumvit. He motioned for me to get in and immediately did a U-turn. Once again, I had been walking in the wrong direction.

We reached Sukhumvit intersection and I recognized that we were much closer to Ekamai Bus Terminal than I had guessed. I handed him the twenty *baht* note and ten *baht* coin I had been holding. Usually I don't make eye contact with the driver and exit the vehicle as quickly as possible. This time though, he did not take his hand away and I noticed he was looking at me.
"Here we go," I thought. "What is it this time?"
"I know. There will be a surcharge because it is after ten o'clock. Or will it be a special tax because it is raining? Because I am overweight there is the additional wear and tear on the vinyl seat plus it will be double fare for the extra fuel he's consumed."

But no, my mental ravings were well off the mark. He handed me back the ten *baht* coin saying, "Only twenty *baht*." You could have knocked me down with a feather. My immediate reaction was that I wanted to throw my arms around him and give him a big hug. Thankfully I resisted the temptation as something told me he may take the gesture the wrong way and I could end up with a new 'best friend'.

My next idea was to thank him very much and tell him to keep the ten *baht*. But, if I did that, it would be a signal he should always charge foreigners the extra money. Obviously foreigners don't care about it. Too many *fa-lung* do this already and it makes life difficult for the rest of us who cannot afford the luxury of tipping all the time. I blame Americans.

Then I thought about giving him a big bonus, maybe one hundred *baht*, and telling him it was a gift for being so honest. Oh, what the hell, I wanted to take him out to dinner! I wanted to marry his daughter and I didn't care how ugly she was.

But I did none of that. I simply accepted the ten *baht*, thanked him very much and walked away. The rain did not annoy me any more and I was overcome by a feeling of well-being that stayed with me for the next couple of days.

It is like my golf game. To say I play golf badly is a gross understatement. But I still play now and then because of one thing that keeps me going. Once in every two hundred strokes (average score for nine hours of playing eighteen holes), I will hit a magnificent shot. It will fly straight, true, long and perfect. This gives me hope and I will forget all about the other hundred or so atrocious shots I played that day. I retrieve my golf clubs from the water hazard, straighten out the ones that I bent around a tree and, playing on, continue to disgrace the noble game.

That *tuk-tuk* driver gave me similar hope. The hope that not all taxi drivers were dishonest low-life's and, in a country where honesty, ethics, sincerity and courtesy seem to be in short supply, there are some decent people to be found.

A few days later, it happened that my favourite shirt was in need of repair. The stitching around the bottom of the pocket had come undone leaving a large hole. My pen kept falling through and I had to decide whether to keep buying more pens or have the pocket re-stitched once and for all.

Close to my apartment, an old lady sits behind a treadle sewing machine. I see her every day and decided to give her the job. I handed her my shirt and pointed out the problem. Nodding, she took the shirt and began searching through her sewing box.

"*Hah na-tee.*"

A few moments later and the shirt was repaired. I looked at the excellent stitch work and noticed that the cotton she used was exactly the same colour as the original. In fact, you could not tell the shirt had been repaired. I guessed the cost would be about twenty *baht*.

"How much?" I asked.

"*Nit noy.* For you – free," came her reply.

Once again, I could not believe what I was hearing. The job was such a snap for her she did not want to charge me for it. I thanked her very much and made a mental note that she had won all future contracts for my clothing repairs. I decided against a marriage proposal because, well, she was really, really old.

In terms of a financial bonus for me the ten *baht* and the twenty *baht* were insignificant. But in terms of goodwill and restoration of my faith in Thai people, the *tuk-tuk* driver and the old seamstress did more for their country than all the glossy tourist brochures ever could. Little did they realize I would retell their story over and over again and now, in print, it will be read by millions. Ok, hundreds.

26

Pattaya Dreaming

ll I ever seem to be doing is talking about Pattaya, sex, girls and drinking. Since these, apart from the latter, are the topics I know least about, it always seemed appropriate that I share my ignorance with the rest of you. Now, I've decided to impart some culcha.

To many of us, poetry consists of five-lines of iambic pentameter beginning with, "There was a young girl from Nantucket." But poetry is much more than that. I often sit in awe at the genius and talent behind the great poets of this world. Admittedly I'm usually shit-face drunk at the time and almost all of my favourite poets are dead, but what the hell, I've usually got nothing better to do. The sonnets of Shakespeare, the verse of Coleridge, Tennyson, Byron, Shelley and the unashamedly Australian satire of Henry Lawson and A.B. (Banjo) Paterson never fail to send shivers down my spine as I read.

In my opinion, modern poetry, i.e. written over the last ten to twenty years, just can not compete. Here's a tip for anyone thinking of writing poetry. It's gotta rhyme. If it doesn't rhyme, it's not poetry! Don't believe the bullshit the English professors tell you about 'free verse'. If you can't make it rhyme, you are simply a prose writer and your contemporary, free verse, mind-numbing ramblings are a load of crap that nobody but you understands. Another tip: When writing poetry, never end a line with the word 'purple'.

In contrast, for those non-Australians reading this, find a copy of A.B. (Banjo) Paterson's 'Man From Snowy River'. If reading that doesn't make the hairs on the back of your neck stand up, nothing will. Without giving too much away, his description of the horse chase is brilliant - and it rhymes!

But back to Pattaya and my favourite Australian poet, Henry Lawson. I wrote a story about a trip to my girlfriend's village and called it, 'Up The County', after one of Henry Lawson's most popular poems. Far be it from me to say I could improve on this poem, but, with a few word changes I think I can make it apply to Pattaya. Here goes:

***

I am back from up the country - very sorry that I went
Seeking for my girlfriend's tribal lands whereon to pitch my tent.
I have shattered many illusions, which were broken on the track,
Spent a lot of hard-earned money, and I'm glad that I am back.
I had my wallet emptied and my Visa card stripped bare,
So she's got another thing coming if she thinks I'm going back there.
I'm happy to stay at present at a boarding house in town,
Drinking beer and Mekong whisky, taking stock and calming down.

Pattaya! What a place! – choked with motorbikes and cars
With its never-ending road works blocking entrances to bars!
Streets of desperation, filled with vendor's high-pitched cries,
Where the looney baht bus driver starts and stares with reddened eyes.
Where, in clouds of smoke enveloped, roasted taxi drivers dash
Swiftly past the sun-shy bar girl dragged behind her source of cash.
With her face simply gleaming, like an aria unsung
His money's quickly leaving, borne aloft her lying tongue.

Miles and miles of quick thirst-quenchers, strings of seedy watering-holes
And air-conditioned bar rooms, offering rest for weary souls.
And women, beautiful women! With their ever-maddening plea
Of "Come in sexy man! – I will go with you for free!"
But that's where charity endeth, and the traveler soon finds out

Nothing! – Nothing is for free, while there's fa-lung about.
Lonely men with hope eternal, believing all their spiel
Forget the primal tenet, that nothing here is real.

Treacherous scams that trap the stranger, endless lies that reap despair,
Dark and sultry-looking women, hiding secrets here and there!
And stories flow like rivers, but when all is said and done,
The truth will come to surface - that money's number one.
Town of grey and shady practice – nothing here is black or white,
For the lost and lonely pilgrim, nor the creatures of the night.
Dismal city for the lover, when the shades begin to rise
On the sad heartbreaking truth, lost beneath the town's disguise.

Dreary town in rainy weather, with the endless clouds that drift
O'er the city like a blanket that the Lord will never lift.
Dismal town when it is raining - streets flood and, oh, the smell
Of the dirty water rising, from the precipice of hell.
Ghastly tunes fill lonely bar rooms where the hapless guest is seated
Forced by rain to keep on drinking, till his money is depleted.

Town where gaunt and street-wise women ply their trade and work the den,
Till their boyfriends, gone out drinking, will return to them again.
Stools of fools overflowing, with a plastic atmosphere,
Where you're asked to buy a lady drink, before you've even got your beer.
Home of tragedy applauded by the bar room's dismal bell,
Heaven of the many - for others, such a hell.
And her roof is always leaking, and the buffalo's mai sabai
And the unsuspecting new-chum falls for each and every lie!

So I am back in Pattaya City, very happy to be here
With a smiling girl beside me and in my hand a beer;
I am under no illusions about what keeps her on my arm,
It's all my hard-earned money, certainly not my looks or charm.
I believe the Pattaya bar girl's dream will not materialize
Till she deals with people fairly and forgets all about the lies.
So I intend to take things slowly and keep my head and lust apart,
Keep my money in my pocket and distance it from my heart.

Pattaya Dreaming   A Fool In Paradise

On a lighter note, first published in *Children of the Bush* in 1902, the poem 'Shearer's Dream' is usually attributed to Henry Lawson and appears in many collections of the poet's works. The following 'Pattaya version' is based upon that poem so I take no credit for it apart from a sick imagination in changing, surprisingly, very few of the words.

O I dreamt I went to a Go Go Bar
And it was a dream of joy,
For every girl was a beauty queen
And not one of them a katoey.
Undressed like girls from a Playboy spread,
The prettiest ever seen,
They had flaxen hair, they had coal black hair
And every shade between.
There was short plump girls, there was tall slim girls
And the handsomest ever seen,
They was four foot two, they was five foot six
And every height between.

The room was cooled by air con vents
That was over every hatch,
The bar was of polished mahogany
And everything else to match.
The couch was one long water bed
And the view was simply grand,
As every night on the floodlit stage
The girls danced to a four-piece band.

Our drinks was free during 'Happy Hour'
So we drank till all was blue,
The girls was washed before they came out
And their bodies was scented too.
And we all of us cried when the lights cut out
In spite of our drunken daze,
For every minute them girls waltzed around
With whisky and beer on trays.

146

There was three of them girls to every chap
And as jealous as they could be,
There was three of them girls to every chap
And six of them picked on me.
We was drafting them out for the homeward track
And sharing them round like cream,
When I woke with my head in the blazing sun
To find it a Pattaya dream.

27

As Old As You Feel

T he other day I was sitting in my favourite Go Go Bar having a
soothing draft beer. I am not what you would call a Go Go Bar
addict, preferring the open-air beer bars to the dimly-lit,
claustrophobic pressure-cookers that some Go Go Bars can be. But I
liked this particular Go Go Bar and had been a regular customer there
for more than two years. When I say 'like' and 'regular customer', the
truth is you could find me there six out of seven nights a week.

The atmosphere is congenial, the girls all know me and they all know
my girlfriend. In fact, sometimes I think they prefer talking with her
than with me. I can joke around with them and they never pressure me
for lady-drinks. The word has probably spread that I never buy a drink
for any girl who asks me for one. The music is actual music, none of
that thump-thump-thump techno crap, the beer is reasonably priced and
there is a free pool table. Any time I wander in there, I know I can get
a cold beer, fun conversation and someone to play pool with. The
place has become my 'Cheers'.

The strange thing about Go Go Bars is that, even though they are not
everyone's cup of tea, some *fa-lung* must be very picky. Time and time
again, I notice a potential customer poke his head through the curtains,
look around the room and then leave without so much as a "hello". My
mate calls them Go Go Bar Inspectors. These guys patrol the *sois* of

Pattaya looking for signs saying 'Go Go Bar'. As soon as they find one, they peer inside: Scantily clad girls dancing on stage? Check. Music playing? Check. Disco lighting? Check. Beer being served? Check. Ok, this one is a Go Go Bar. Time to move on and investigate the next one.

I cannot work out what these guys want. What do they hope to find? What could they possibly see from the doorway that would actually tempt them to come in and sit down? Anyone who can answer that question may be able to make some money here in Pattaya.

But this story is not about the quirks of the tourists nor what makes the perfect Go Go Bar. This particular evening, I was quietly sipping my beer when a new customer came through the door. He was not one of the Go Go Bar Inspectors and was being escorted by the girl whose job it is to sit outside and entice new punters inside. Scarcely through the curtains, one of the dancers on her break came over to his other side and helped him to a seat. The reason for the assistance was that he was at least eighty years old, going on a hundred. He was not fat but walked, or shuffled, with the aid of one of those walking sticks with a tripod base.

Once comfortably seated, the service girl went to get his drink and the dancer stayed by his side. When she came back with his beer, the service girl then left to return to her post at the entrance. Another dancer, also on her break, came and sat at his other side. I sat back and admired the sight of a man in his eighties flanked by two beautiful, practically naked, girls in their early twenties. And he was enjoying himself. He was chatting away with both of them, they were giggling and he never stopped smiling.

I tried not to stare but could not help watching him. The scene made me feel warm inside. It made me think about his alternatives. I don't know what nationality he was but his lifestyle in his home country could not possibly be anything like this. Back there, I guess his daily choices consisted of whether to do cross-stitch or play dominos with some boring geriatric in a nursing home. Then some patronizing male nurse would come along with the day's major consideration – whether to have creamed rice or custard with his stewed prunes.

Here, sitting in the Go Go Bar, his choices were obvious and sitting either side of him. He could allow one, or both, of the playful young things to pamper him, he could buy them drinks or he could do exactly what he was doing and that was enjoying their company and attention. Each time one of the girls returned to the stage to dance, another one replaced her at his side. And he smiled.

As she passed on her way to the stage, I joked with one of the girls. "You want *boomsing* old man?"
She replied in Thai that no, she would probably not '*boomsing*' him because she was scared he might die. There it was in a nutshell. Her consideration was not that he was older than her grandfather, nor was it that the man could hardly walk. It was the fear that, in the throws of passion, he may have a heart attack.

What a wonderful place this Pattaya is. The detractors, moralists and meddlers can rant and rave all they like but what I witnessed was a man in his twilight years enjoying himself. His companions were enjoying his company also. If they weren't, they would get up and leave. For all their pretence, it is a fact that, money or no money, many bar girls will not stay with a man if they do not like him. I unfortunately know one *fa-lung* in Pattaya who is so obnoxious he finds it difficult to get a girl he knows, or knows of him, to sit with him for five minutes.

The joke goes that a man is only as old as the woman he feels. Well, this guy was feeling about twenty-two years old. And if he had chosen to be further entertained, I am certain he could have enticed one of the bubbly young ladies to take good care of him. Then, if the unfortunate happened, whereas I would feel sorry for the girl because she may harbour thoughts that she contributed to his death, I would not feel sorry for him. He would have shuffled off his mortal coil the way I would want to, and not laying in a bed surrounded by greedy relatives, copies of his Will in their hands, telling the doctor to "pull the plug". At least in Pattaya he would have gone with a smile on his face.

28

Worm Writing

There should come a time when foreigners living in Thailand and frequent visitors decide they would be far better off to learn to speak the language. I say 'should' because it appears that there are two groups of foreigners who don't agree – Americans and Brits. Americans believe that everyone on the planet can understand their novel version of the English language as long as they speak it LOUDLY and s-l-o-w-l-y! Many Brits on the other hand seem to retain a Gunboat mentality, believing the rest of the world should learn the Queen's English. The rest of us persevere knowing full well that no matter how hard we try, we will never be able to get our tongues around some of the words the Thais find so easy to verbalize.

Being one of those people who prefers to understand what is going on around him, I bought yet another 'teach yourself' Thai book. I have found these books helpful in the past when I simply wished to learn some basic phrases. Unfortunately, the seven books I now have in my library do not really teach the language. To seriously learn grammar and sentence construction, I know that I should attend classes with a fully qualified Thai teacher, but I am a Cheap Charlie. For now, at least, I rely on the books to find the words or phrases and my girlfriend to help with the pronunciation. It is enough for me to be able to communicate most of my needs to the relevant portion of the local population.

In his introduction to the book, the author noted that many students of Thai merely wanted to learn conversation because the Thai alphabet and writing system looked too difficult. He went on to say it was a big mistake to think this way. Being able to read Thai develops speaking and listening skills and students of the language should wean themselves off transliteration as soon as possible. I was of the opinion that learning to read and write a language that has forty-four consonants, thirty-two vowel combinations and five tones was a bit out of my depth. My friend Frank called it 'worm writing' and with all its circles and squiggles, it is easy to see why.

But, the author whet my appetite and I had plenty of time on my hands. I was also having trouble trying to pronounce Thai words using the Anglicized version given in the text books. It seemed each writer devised his own method of writing the different sounds and I was forever being forced to refer back to the glossary at the front of the book to check if I was pronouncing the word correctly. For example, the transliteration of the Thai word for 'can' or 'able to' was shown, in various texts, as *dai*, *dy*, *daai* and *da:i*.

So, with no reason not to, I started learning to read and write Thai. As far as being able to understand more of the spoken language, it was a good decision. As far as being able to pronounce the words correctly, it was of even greater help. Although spelling will always be a problem, to those of you who are not convinced that, as well as learning to speak Thai you should at least learn to read it, I can report it is well worth the effort and not as difficult as it first looks.

For a start, of the forty-four consonants in the Thai alphabet, three are obsolete and another half dozen are so rarely used they are not worth worrying about. Of the thirty-two vowel combinations, many of the sounds seem to repeat, although I know Thais can differentiate between each one. There are no capital letters in the Thai system and, whether handwritten or printed, the letters all appear the same size. Words run together but most writers place a gap between sentences. There are usually no commas, full stops or other punctuation marks except for question and quotation marks.

152

In no time at all, I found myself able to look at text and break the sentences up into individual words. It became clear where one word ended and another began. Actually, I should say 'syllable' instead of 'word'. Some of the multi-syllabic words still give me problems but I can make a very close approximation of the sound of each component.

It was illuminating but became a double-edged sword. I enjoyed learning, but the 'official' way of transliteration from Thai to English began to annoy me. Foreigners, including myself, rely upon the experts getting it right. This is particularly important when it comes to translating place names. Tourists, by definition, tour, and they rely on maps and guides to help them get around. Sometimes it becomes necessary to ask local people for directions. Winston Churchill once stated, "Everybody has a right to pronounce foreign names as he chooses." Obviously he never tried backpacking through Thailand. If a tourist cannot correctly pronounce the name of the place he wishes to visit, his task is made extremely difficult.

In my humble opinion, the official transliteration of Thai into English is wrong. One example is Sukhumvit Road. When have you heard a Thai pronounce this word as it is written in English? For a start, there is no 'v' in Thai. There is no letter that even sounds remotely like a 'v'. Reading the word 'Sukhumvit', I would pronounce it suck – hum – vit, which is incorrect. It should be pronounced as soo (as in sook), koom (sounding like 'come' spoken with a Cockney accent), and wit (as in halfwit). The last syllable begins with a 'w', not a 'v'.

The official transliteration uses 'th' to indicate a true 't' sound as opposed to a 't' to indicate a sound half way between a 't' and a 'd'. Similarly it uses 'ph' to indicate a true 'p' sound and a 'p' to indicate half way between a 'p' and a 'b'. I have a novel idea! Why not use a 't' to denote a true 't', a 'dt' to denote a sound half way between a 'd' and a 't', a 'p' to indicate a true 'p' and a 'bp' to indicate a sound half way between a 'b' and a 'p'? Too difficult? Too radical?

The word 'Pattaya' is misspelled and mispronounced so often it becomes irritating. One signpost on the road from Bangkok has it beginning with 'Ph'. Translating directly from the Thai, it should be written as Putayah. Showing the syllables – Put-a-yah. It should be pronounced 'put' like a golf putt, followed by a very short 'a' and a very long 'yah'.

Another example is a town well known to expats who have done visa runs to Cambodia. Located in the south east corner of Thailand, Trat is how it is written on the maps, but try asking a Thai if they have ever heard of it. By my transliteration, it should be written as 'Dt-r-a-h-t'. The first letter is a cross between a 'd' and a 't'. But, here's the rub. As in the English language, Thai has some words in which a letter is silent. In this case, the 'r' is silent. Thus the town should be pronounced 'Dtaht', to rhyme with *baht*.

The official transliteration of the Thai word for 'foreigner' is farang. Since writing the book, *'Money Number One'*, I have received some criticism for writing the word as *fa-lung*. To those critics, I make no apology. My hearing receptors must be different to theirs because I have never heard a Thai pronounce the word as 'farang'.

The word is comprised of two syllables. The first is 'fa', – very short vowel sound as if you were going to say the word 'fun' without the 'n'. The second syllable is 'rung', the same as a rung on a ladder. It is not 'rang' as in "I rang the bell". The spelling *farung* would be more correct and will be spoken by upper class Bangkok Thais, well-educated Thais, Thai singers and Thai newsreaders. However, the majority of Thais have trouble pronouncing an 'r' at the beginning of a syllable and pronounce it as an 'l' instead. This means most of the Thais I speak with will pronounce the word *'fa-lung'* and therefore so do I. I use the hyphen to separate the syllables.

Most irritating is when some English speakers use the word *'farangs'* when referring to more than one foreigner. This is doubly offensive to my selectively pedantic soul because there are no plural words in Thai and no Thai word ever ends with an 's'. I say 'selectively' because if you wish to be strictly pedantic, there is no such word as Thais either, when referring to more than one Thai person. The words *'fa-lung'* or

154

'*farung*', as well as the word 'Thai', are both singular and plural. Much like the English word 'sheep'.

Unfortunately, I have become used to using the word 'Thais' when referring to more than one Thai person. I use it in everyday speech and in everything I have written. So I am just going to have to put up with it, even though, with my newfound knowledge, I know it to be incorrect.

In the English language, the letter 'c' changes its sound depending on the letter following it. E.g. cat; church; cereal. Many Thai consonants change their sound depending on whether they are at the beginning or the end of a syllable. For example, there are four Thai consonants equivalent to 's' in English. At the end of a syllable, they are all pronounced as a 't'. The one Thai letter equivalent to 'r' as well as the two letters equivalent to 'l' change to an 'n' at the end of a syllable and the four 'd's change to 't's.

Because of this unusual feature of the language, if you exclude words ending with 'w' or 'y', which are actually vowel sounds, there are only six consonant sounds at the end of words or syllables – 'k', 'm', 'n', 'ng', 'p' and 't'. This is why Thai people have difficulty pronouncing many English words, particularly those ending in 's', 'th', 'ch', 'l', 'f' and 'd'. As if a great weight had been lifted from my shoulders, I understand why I always receive a 'bin' instead of a 'bill' at the end of the evening.

Adopting my role as a true smartarse, I used to sit and read Thai newspapers aloud for my girlfriend. Although probably sounding to her delicate Thai ears like Jed Clampett reciting Shakespeare, she pretended to be very impressed and complained that I *roo mahk* [know too much]. What she didn't realize was that ninety-nine percent of the time, I did not have a clue what I was reading.

29

Out of the Mouths of Babes

O ne of the great things about living in a foreign country is the communication gap. Yes, at times it can be frustrating not being able to get your point across effectively but mostly, if you have a sense of humour, it can be a lot of fun. Colloquialisms aside, the gap between intention, delivery and comprehension can be a constant source of amusement, no more so than in Pattaya. What follows is a collection of the best one-liner's I have heard since being in Pattaya. Most names, of course, have been changed.

I was watching a war movie on television when my girlfriend came and sat beside me. She watched the action for a few moments then remarked, "Oh, big fighting." Feeling the need to explain to her a little of what was going on, I answered in bamboo English, "This World War Two. Happen sixty years ago. England, Australia and America fighting Japan and Thailand."

"Oh," she said, her eyes bulging at hearing the word 'Thailand'.

"Who win?"

(Thailand was an ally of Japan during World War II and actually declared war on Great Britain, America and Australia.)

Alan was standing at a bar when one of the girls approached and rubbed his rotund stomach. "Have baby," she said, to which Alan's standard reply was, "Yes, have Heineken baby." She shook her head and continued to rub. "No. I think you not have Heineken baby – have Heineken family!"

There is the well-worn out yarn about the guy who was having an argument with his bar girl girlfriend. She didn't seem to understand why he was so angry. "But you lied to me!" he shouted. She looked back at him with a puzzled expression. "That's my job!" she replied.

The bar girl looked across at him saying, "If you pay bar fine for me, I think I win lottery." Before he could bask in his newfound glory, she continued, "But when I wake up tomorrow, I think I lose ticket."

The phone rang at Larry's bar and the girl handed it to him simply saying, "*fa-lung*." Larry said, "hello" and the voice on the other end said, "It's John from Birmingham. Is *Noy* there?" Larry looked around and could see no other staff other than the girl who handed him the phone.

"No, not at the moment."

The voice continued, "Please tell her that I am on a plane and we are ready to land at Bangkok airport. I will catch a taxi straight to Pattaya and I'll see her in a few hours."

"Ok, not a problem."

Larry hung up but then remembered that there were two girls named *Noy* working in his bar. When one of them arrived some time later, he asked her if she knew John from Birmingham. Never heard of him. When the other *Noy* turned up, he asked her. After a moment of deep concentration, she smiled and said that he was her English boyfriend. Larry, who could speak no Thai, then tried to pass on the message. Pointing to the heavens, he said that John was on a plane coming into Bangkok and he will see her in a few hours. Smiling excitedly, she ran outside to the road, looked up into the sky and asked, "Where?"

Chatting to a girl in a Beer Bar early one evening, the expat decided to cut to the chase. He asked her if she preferred to go ';short time' or 'long time'. She looked him squarely in the eyes and replied, "Ino want 'short time', no want 'long time' - I want '*life* time'!"

One afternoon, I was walking alone along side of the road to *Jomtien* Beach when a snake came out of the bushes and slithered across the path in front of me. It was about a metre long, lime-green in colour and I don't think that it represented any real danger to me. I stopped until it passed out of sight.

On returning to my apartment, I spoke of the incident to my Thai girlfriend. She smiled with excitement and joyfully explained that, in Thailand, this was considered to be a sign of very good luck indeed. I could not help myself. I asked her what if the snake had turned around and bitten me. "Oh," she said, her face now very serious, "that would be (considered to be a sign of) very bad luck!"

In the 'a stupid question deserves a stupid answer' department, a starry-eyed *fa-lung* once asked his bar girl companion, "Do you really love me?" Without hesitation she replied, "Up to you!"

The guy bought his long-time girlfriend a motorbike. And she was happy. One day she returned to the condo in a very aggitated state, telling him that a policeman had stopped her and demanded 400 *baht*.
"Ahh, you weren't wearing your helmet again," he laughed. "But I thought the fine was only 200 *baht*?"
"Yes, but I not have license."
"You forgot to take your license with you?"
"Not forget. I no have license."
"You what?"
"No problem," she interrupted. "Because I *mao* [drunk], I argue with policeman and only pay 200 *baht*."

But not all the noteworthy conversation comes out of the mouths of the babes in the bars, some emanates from babes in the woods.

The group of *fa-lung* were talking about their girlfriends or, should I say, problems with their girlfriends. The general agreement was that the girls were very demanding and costing them a fortune. One guy shocked his friends by stating that, "My girlfriend never asks me for anything."

"Gee, mate, you've really got a good one then," was the general response.

"Sure have. She simply finds my wallet, takes the money out and buys whatever she wants! Never asks."

It was the first night of his first trip to Thailand and he was sitting at a Pattaya Beer Bar. One of the bar girls, keen to meet a new customer, pulled out the stool beside him, sat down and gave him a welcoming smile. Greetings were exchanged and they shook hands. Once he had his drink in front of him, he worked up the courage to ask her name. A few more pleasantries in broken English to cut the ice and then he brought the house down. In all sincerity and naivete he asked her, "and what do you do for a living?"

It seems that the first night in Pattaya is the ultimate culture shock. This guy was not as naive as the previous one, because he worked out the score quite early in the piece. Or did he? On his first night he was chatting up one lovely young lady who seemed quite willing. He was intrigued though when she asked him, "Do you like lady smoke?" Being a non-smoker himself, he truthfully replied that no, he did not like a lady who smoked. She became somewhat disinterested after that and he ended up going back to his hotel alone.

The next evening he went to a different bar. One lady he was rather keen on, during the course of their limited conversation, again asked, "You like lady smoke?" As with the previous night, he replied in the negative but started to wonder what the predisposition for women who smoked was all about. Again, he went home alone.

On the third night, when the question came up, he replied yes, it was alright if the lady smoked, figuring that a change of answer may give him more success than he had been getting. It worked and he bar fined the girl. That night, back in his hotel room, he found out the Pattaya meaning of the term 'smoke'.

A long time Pattaya visitor and his girlfriend partied heavily on his first night back in town. By midnight they were both extremely drunk, she being the worst affected. He carried her back to their hotel room where she proceeded to empty the contents of her stomach just before reaching the bathroom. He cleaned her up as best he could, left her on the bed and decided to get back to the bar and continue partying with his mates.

By 4:00am, he decided to call it a night but forgot his room number. He did not want to approach the hotel reception staff because he was in no condition to speak coherently. He called his girlfriend's mobile to ask what the room number was.

"*Be sik o' foor,*" she drowsily replied.
"Yes, I know you were sick on the floor. What is the room number?"
"*You come now. Be sik o' foor,*"
"I know you were sick. I was there! Now what is my room number?"
"*Be sik o' foor,*" she repeated.
With that he gave up. He called her stupid and hung up. Instead of going back to his hotel, he booked a room in one near where he was drinking.

The next afternoon he returned to his original hotel to confront his girlfriend. He was furious but changed his tune once he asked the girl at reception what his room number was.
"B-6-0-4," came her reply.

30

The Secret Policemen's Ball

"Man seeks to escape himself in myth, and does so by any
means at his disposal. Drugs, alcohol, or lies. Unable to
withdraw into himself, he disguises himself. Lies and
inaccuracy give him a few moments of comfort."
Jean Cocteau (1889–1963), French author, filmmaker.

The *Pattaya Trader* magazine of December 2002 carried an article by my good friend Duncan Stearn entitled, "Will the real Baron von Munchausen please stand up." The piece was about the many foreigners in Pattaya who 'reinvent themselves' and end up sitting in bars telling tall tales untrue from their legendary pasts. It seems to be more than a coincidence that most of them have worked for, or are still working for, pseudo-paramilitary organizations, quasi-law enforcement agencies or the miss-intelligence communities. Not one of them is a retired filing clerk from the Department of Motor Vehicles.

As Duncan implied in his article, these guys have probably been watching too many James Bond movies. I would have suggested they have been reading too many spy thrillers but, for most of them, literacy would be too much to ask for.

I feel obliged to add my two *baht*'s worth because, the evening after reading Duncan's article, I was sitting at a bar. An acquaintance introduced me to an acquaintance of his, who it just so happened, worked for Interpol. Well, not Interpol as such, but a branch of Interpol, which he could not name because it was a secret. P-lease!

Two weeks later, it again happened I was sitting in a bar chatting with my friend, the American owner. Being an American-run bar, it sports a large US flag displayed prominently at the entrance. In walked a new customer. He was about forty years old, tall, neatly dressed and alone. What made me notice him was that, as he passed the US flag, he kissed his hand then placed it on the flag. "Here we go," I thought as he sat down at our table.

In his first sentence he introduced himself, expressed concern that he had no money, asked my friend if he could borrow one hundred *baht* and swore he would return the money later that evening with the words "you have the word of a United States Navy Seal on that!" I wanted to ask him if that meant he could balance a beach ball on his nose, but I resisted the urge. My friend gave him the money as I turned away to hide the fact that I was stifling laughter.

It turned out he was a former US Navy Seal - a point he mentioned more than fifty times over the next half hour - and was temporarily down on his luck. His speech and mannerisms reminded me of the movie *Men In Black*. In the interview scene, when the candidates were asked why they were there, one uniformed guy sprung to his feet, stood at attention, clicked his heels and replied, "because you are looking for the best of the best of the best, sir!"

But the best was yet to come. Before he left, presumably to get the money to repay my friend, he mentioned that the day before, he had been to the US Embassy in Bangkok where he was sworn in by the CIA. My friend was not amused when I sprayed my mouthful of beer over the nice clean bar top. He went on to say that 'they' had not yet informed him exactly what his mission was going to be, but he was waiting for 'the call'. I suspect 'they' had actually given him his orders but the piece of paper self-destructed before he could finish reading it. The world is eternally grateful.

Over the next couple of weeks I was informed that there is a group of French Foreign Legionnaires in town who should not be messed with. Apparently, these guys are so tough they can crack a man's skull with only a stare. There is also a guy from the Bulgarian Secret Police working undercover in Pattaya. He is easily recognizable because he always carries an umbrella.

Another Pattaya resident, unfortunately an Australian, is the world's greatest conspiracy theorist. He makes Mel Gibson's character in the movie *Conspiracy Theory* look positively sane. He is convinced ASIO (Australian Security Intelligence Organization) is out to get him. He dare not return to Australia because he believes he would not make it out of the airport alive. When he talks to you, he stands really close so that the voice-detecting ray guns being aimed at his mouth cannot pick up what he is saying. I suspect he lines the inside of his hat with aluminium foil so that the spy satellites cannot send down a laser beam to fry his brains. Too late.

What information this guy may possess that could possibly be a threat to any nation's security is beyond me. As far as his special talents go, the only likelihood is he was trained by a foreign power as an operative whose task it is to seek out government agents, get close to them and bore them to death.

He has made contingency plans to cover all eventualities but is concerned about using the fake passport he made for himself. Due to a leak within his own security network, he is certain alarm bells will ring at ASIO Headquarters once a Mr. M. Mouse tries to pass through Australian Immigration.

But the Oscar goes to the guy who can be seen from time to time dancing, prancing and slobbering around Central Pattaya. This guy looks like he just came out of the trees and then only because the monkeys threw him out. Not so, according to the 120 kilogram Australian Federal Policeman on assignment in Pattaya sitting beside me at the bar. I was informed the guy was actually a very intelligent man who only pretended to be the totally insane fruit-loop I took him to be. He is working undercover for the Pattaya police and reporting on illegal activity. That was fake saliva dripping down his chin and the odour permeating from his body was in fact sprayed from a can – Eau de Sewer – each morning to reinforce his masquerade. Well, there you go.

Pattaya, it seems, is also full of 'sleepers' and 'moles' who can be seen each morning reading the *Bangkok Post* Personal column. They are not searching for a mate, but checking to see if there is a coded message for them to be reactivated into service. "John Brown – all is forgiven. Please call home. Mum." If World War III ever breaks out, more than one half of the foreigners in Pattaya will be called back into the service of their respective countries. The *Post's* Personal column that day will run into three full pages and telephone boxes throughout the city will suddenly be taken over by overweight, middle-aged foreign men talking into their shoes.

But in all seriousness, I feel it my duty to pass on a message to the Human Resource Managers of MI5, 6, 7 and 8, the CIA, B, C and D, the SAS, GAS, Mossad, Tossad, Interpol, Intercourse and Control. Guys, a reassessment of your recruitment and selection processes is urgently required. The agents you are hiring now are all blabbermouths. Not one of them can keep his mouth shut long enough to keep a secret. And they don't have to be tortured. Most don't even have to be drunk.
"How's your beer, mate?"
"I work for the CIA."
"That's nice."

My brother lived and worked in Bangkok twelve years ago. He once told me all the secret agents used to meet in Patpong. They would wander up and down Patpong 1 and 2, ducking into Go Go Bars now and then in order to lose anyone who may be following them. Once they had shaken off any tail, they would enter Mizu's Japanese restaurant, go upstairs, order a sizzling steak and pass secret messages under the table. And I thought he was joking.

31

Year of Living Stupidly

Today is my birthday. As has been the case for the last fifteen years or so, this is not a day for celebration. Each year, for the week preceding my birthday, I become morose, depressed, catatonic, gin and tonic, homicidal, suicidal and generally not much fun to be around. It is also a time for reflection and I use the day to look back over the previous year and list my achievements, failures, the lessons I have learned, the mistakes I have made, the trials and the tribulations.

Being a very methodical person, I take out two pieces of paper, mark one 'The Good' and the other 'The Bad'. I compile a list under each heading and compare where I am now to where I was twelve months ago. Alas, the result is always the same and each year for the past fifteen years, the conclusion drawn is that I am slipping further and further down the food-chain.

I am in relatively good health. That's a 'good'. During the past year I have not been run down by a *baht* bus though not through lack of trying on the part of the drivers. I feel certain if I keep handing over only five *baht* for my fare, the *baht* bus mafia will eventually put a contract out on my miserable hide. I have not fallen off, nor under the wheels of, marauding motorcycles yet. One did sideswipe my chair while I was sitting in a restaurant. The rider simply smiled and assured me he would have another go next time he sees me in a supermarket.

I have put on a few kilos and lost some hair, with more and more of the remaining follicles taking it upon themselves to change colour from baby-shit brown to a nuclear fallout grey. My eyesight is deteriorating exponentially and although my long vision is still good, my short vision is such that I will either have to get reading glasses or longer arms. (My school's religious instruction teacher was right – it *does* make you go blind!)

Unfortunately, my good health only refers to my physical state. The same cannot be said about my mental health. That's a 'bad'. Human beings are supposed to become wiser with age but unfortunately, someone forgot to tell my gene pool. I just seem to be getting sillier by the day and I am turning into a used car salesman's dream. This, of course, is very good news for a number of ailing buffaloes scattered throughout the Kingdom.

I am now in Pattaya. That's a 'good'. But I am living nowhere near the standard at which I would like to be accustomed. It is like being at a Fun Fair where the cheapest ride is a shilling and only having eleven pence halfpenny in your pocket. (For American readers: "where the cheapest ride is a dollar and you only have three quarters and two nickels in your pocket.") That's a 'bad'. Living modestly and trying to make each *baht* stretch is not the lifestyle I had envisaged. Even though the cost of living here is low, really enjoying Pattaya requires the egress of plenty of the folding stuff. Sure, I can stay away from the bars and therefore save a lot of money. But that is the whole point of living in Pattaya – the nightlife. Take that away and I may as well be living in any other city in any other country in the world. B-o-r-i-n-g.

On the romantic front, I am still living with the same girl I was a year ago, so you could say my love life is going well. That's a 'good'. So far, I can find very little wrong with her. She appears honest and faithful and takes good care of me. If she is a gold-digger, she is digging in the wrong place. Time to replace the batteries in her metal detector. But alas, in all honesty, I am starting to crave the carefree life of a single man again. That's a 'bad'. Life is getting too predictable, too mundane and I just think it is time for a change. Unfortunately, I have not got the heart to tell her about my idea. I just cannot bring myself to do that even though it would be the easiest way out.

I thought of doing a bit of 'butterflying' and letting her catch me at it, but then I know exactly what would happen. After the initial tirade of abuse, my girlfriend would go away for a couple of hours then come back and forgive me. Forgiven, but not forgotten. She would be suspicious of me after that and not want to let me out of her sight. Life could become unbearable.

So what am I complaining about? I have a great relationship. This is in stark contrast to my life back in Australia where the only way I could possibly get a girlfriend under the age of sixty would be to own a house with a swimming pool and look like Mel Gibson. And even if I did manage to get a girlfriend, all I would have to do was say I did not like her new hairstyle, or worse, not notice her new hairstyle, and she would be out the door, never to return.

I must confess that I'm going through yet another mid-life crisis – my fifteenth, in fact – and have started to think about the most absurd things. For instance, never in my life have I purchased my own underwear. Until the time I got married, my mother bought them for me. Once married, it was my wife. Even after the divorce it was a succession of girlfriends or Cheap Charlie female relatives that did the shopping. Just once, I would like to be in charge of the underwear purchasing department! What a bastard. What a mess. That's a 'bad'.

Lastly, there is my financial status to consider. Exactly twelve months ago I was working on a job in Australia that eventually, I did not get paid for. Today, I am still not receiving any income but at least I am not working for it. That's a 'good'. I currently owe more money to more people than ever before in my life. Unfortunately, I also owe money to two financial institutions in Australia. These institutions are comprised of totally unfunny people who are non-sympathetic to the myriad of imaginative excuses I have come up with as to why I cannot pay the money back yet. I have full intentions of coming good with all the money for all the people I owe, but I have to rely on other people to pay me first. These people are sure taking their time about it and seem unconcerned at my financial plight. Frustration building, money ending, suicide pending. That's a 'bad'.

So, today is my birthday. If it is true that you can count the number of people who care about you by the number of birthday greetings you receive, then I have a grand total of one. My *tee-ruk* was the only one who remembered. My three children back in Australia forgot altogether, as did my one and only brother. Not a word from any of them. Last year, my brother sent me an e-mail three days late in which he wished me a happy 44th birthday for the 15th. My birthday falls on the 14th and last year, I turned 45. That's a 'bad'.

To sum up, I look at the two pages of paper in front of me to find that the 'good' total four and the 'bad' total six. Forty percent is not really a displeasing effort and reminds me of my school report cards. One thing I have learned over the years is you should never think to yourself, or say out load, things could not get any worse. Life has a way of showing you that it indeed can get worse. So, to all the Gods out there who may be reading this, I am not unhappy with my lot. In the poker game of life you have dealt me a pair of nines and, in the words of Kenny Rogers, "every hand's a winner and every hand's a loser," it is simply a matter of how one plays the game.

32

Pattaya Quiz

From the first moment a male tourist arrives in Pattaya he is on a learning curve. Sometimes the curve rises sharply and sometimes gradually as he becomes accustomed to the place and the people. At times, riding the curve can be painful and costly but, for most of the time, the journey to become more street-wise is enjoyable.

There are no accurate benchmarks or performance indicators to determine just how good someone is at coping with the Pattaya experience. Although evolution will weed out the truly stupid ones, (missed me so far), no foreign male could ever, or should ever, boast that, "I am so clever, nobody in this town will ever get the better of me." I am living proof that the fastest route to disaster is via the highway of overconfidence.

This is Pattaya, where the sublime becomes the ridiculous, the mundane turns into the exciting and the trivial becomes the complicated. The trick to survival here is not to judge the place by Western standards, don't fight against the system and never try to understand it. You must roll with the punches and not let too many things upset you.

The following questionnaire should enable visitors and guests to determine approximately how much they have learned about Pattaya and, more importantly, what their chances of long-term survival are.

Q1 You and the love of your life have had an argument. You have been living together for one month and she means more to you than life itself. She storms out of the apartment. You

a) run after her, apologizing and begging her not to leave. You finally settle on a two *baht* gold trinket as your peace offering.
b) walk after her, apologizing and asking her to reconsider.
c) yell at her to stay out and not come back until she is ready to apologize.
d) pack her bag while she is out, leave it at reception and change the locks.

Q2 You are marooned on a deserted island with a Pattaya policeman, a twenty-year-old Pattaya bar girl, a fifty-year-old housewife from *Issan* and a recently escaped criminal from one of Thailand's toughest jails. You have a gun with three bullets. Which one do you leave alive?

a) The Policeman, because he is well-trained to serve and protect. You would have a better chance of survival with him looking after you.
b) The bar girl, because you may be stuck on the island for some time and a bar girl companion will keep you comforted.
c) The *Issan* woman, because she will know how to forage for food and to cook. After a while, she may even start to look good.
d) The convict, because at least you KNOW he cannot be trusted.

Q3 It is 8:59pm and you are sitting at a bar in *Soi* 2. One of the other customers is a Norwegian guy, with more money than sense, who insists on ringing the bell every half hour. You are supposed to meet your friends in Walking Street at 9:00pm because they are leaving for home in the morning. You

a) *check bin* immediately, hail a motorcycle taxi and tell the driver that you will give him 100 *baht* to get you to South Pattaya as quickly as possible.

b) *check bin*, walk to Beach Road and catch a *baht* bus to South Pattaya.

c) stay put but feel extremely guilty for being late to meet your friends. You hope they will understand.

d) stay put and time your drinks to last thirty minutes. Friends? What friends?

Q4 You wake up to see the clock beside the bed reads eleven o'clock. You

a) bounce out of bed realizing that the jogging track along Beach Road may already be too crowded.

b) crawl out of bed realizing that you only have two hours to catch the all-you-can-eat- buffet breakfast at the Lek Hotel.

c) realize you are not in your own room because you don't own a clock.

d) What's a clock?

Q5 Your girlfriend tells you that you are drinking too much, eating too much and spending too much time with your mates and not enough time with her. You

a) agree to stop drinking, go on a diet and spend a lot more time with her.

b) agree to ease up on your drinking, watch what you eat and only see your mates three times a week.

c) tell her that it is "up to me".

d) change girlfriends.

Q6   Early one evening you notice a very attractive girl wearing a tight mini skirt sitting side-saddle on the back of a motorcycle taxi. She is putting on her make-up and smiling at you. You

a)   run over to her and mention this was very dangerous and, if the bike was involved in an accident, she could be severely injured.
b)   smile back but continue drinking your beer.
c)   follow her to find out what bar she works in.
d)   walk over to her, give her your mobile number and tell her to call you when she finishes work.

Q7   One night an extremely attractive girl wearing a miniskirt approaches you along the southern end of Beach Road. You

a)   engage her in conversation and suggest you both go for a meal at a nice seafood restaurant.
b)   accept her suggestion you both go back to your room for the night.
c)   keep walking muttering something about already having a girlfriend.
d)   ask him how much for a 'blowie'.

Q8   Your girlfriend invites you to visit her home in the province for a week. You

a)   enthusiastically agree to go, hire a car for seven days and set about buying gifts for her family.
b)   agree to go and ask her what is the best bus to catch, where it leaves from and when.
c)   feign illness.
d)   say no but suggest she go alone. Give her 1,000 *baht* for the trip saying that, if she stays away for a month, you'll give her another 1,000 *baht* as a bonus.

Q9 You are sitting in a Go Go Bar and surrounded by six beautiful dancers. You have bought them all a 'lady drink' and the other dancers on stage are all smiling at you. You

    a) ring the bell, deciding it is easier than buying 'lady drinks' for them all individually.

    b) choose the best four to keep you entertained and buy four more 'lady drinks'.

    c) select the best looking of the bunch and tell her to drink slowly.

    d) wake up realizing this could only be a bad dream.

Q10 Your girlfriend tells you she wants to bring her mother to stay for a month. You say

    a) "Sure, darling, but this apartment is too small. Let's go out today and look for a bigger condo for the three of us."

    b) "Sure, darling, but this apartment is too small. When she comes, I'll rent another room for her."

    c) "I have to go to Finland on business for a month. She can stay with you while I'm gone."

    d) "No!"

Scoring: For every (a) answer, score 0 points; for (b) – 3 points; for (c) – 7 points and for (d) – 10 points.

0-9 You are a walking wallet, an empty Visa card waiting to happen and a prize pigeon ready to be plucked. Leave now while you still have your money and your passport. Better still, come and see me – I have a unique investment opportunity for you.

10-29 You are slightly smarter than stupid but still have a long way to go. This may be your second trip to Pattaya but, in this town, unless you learn the ropes within twenty-four hours, your goose is cooked. Look, listen and learn from graduates of the Pattaya School of Hard Knocks.

30-59 You are at the halfway point. Your future success depends upon how long it took you to reach this stage. If you have only been in Pattaya for a few days, then there is hope. If you have been here for twelve months, then smarten up or catch the next plane home.

60-89 This is potentially the most dangerous category to be in. You think you know it all. You are extremely sure of yourself and listen to other foreigner's tales of misfortune saying something like, "that would never happen to me." You may no longer fall for the obvious traps but you are an easy target for a cunning Pattaya trickster or a beautiful pair of legs.

90-100 You are a hardened Pattaya veteran who has acclimatized too well. You have been in Pattaya for so long you have passed the point of no return. You would not survive back in your own country for more than two minutes - even if you still had your passport and were allowed to return.

33

The Life of Riley

Riley is an American, fifty-nine years old. Twice divorced in his home country, he cannot remember the last time he was in the States. He has been in Thailand for three years following a year or so in Vietnam. Before that was a stint in the Philippines after a long period in Korea. His only claim to fame appeared to be a framed letter, addressed to him, hanging proudly on his wall. The letter was emblazoned with official-looking insignia and stated; "The President of the United States believes that it would serve this Nation's best interests if you would not return in the foreseeable future." It was signed "Jimmy Carter". I have a strong feeling the letter is a fake but he swears it is genuine and becomes aggressive when anyone questions its authenticity.

He lives off a small pension that pays for his monthly rent and food. The pension is a 100% disability type, but how he managed to get it is anyone's guess. He walks, jogs, drinks and indulges the ladies from time to time so, if he is 100% disabled then there are a lot of us out there.

To supplement his pension and thus allow himself to fund a better lifestyle, he dabbles. He dabbles in anything that could possibly earn him a few extra *baht*. He plays the stock market via the internet and, although he did explain to me how it works, my grey matter failed to understand a word he was saying. He boasted that over the past year he had averaged a profit of US$400 per month. Not a bad effort, really. Sustainable? Who knows.

When I last saw him he was beaming and it was obvious he was dying to tell me something. Over a beer, he produced his latest pride and joy. He had just got his first Thai driver's license. I asked him which packet of cornflakes did he get it out of but he was adamant it was the real thing.

He went to the driver's license issuing centre with all the paper work necessary for his application. It would cost 500 *baht* he was told. This was the special *'fa-lung* price'. For Thais, the fee was 100 *baht*. Here was the old double standard two-tiered pricing again and it was a constant point of annoyance for Riley.

"If they tried that in the States," he would say, "there would be a hundred lawyers breathing down their necks in ten seconds flat and they'd lock them up faster than you could say 'throw away the key!'"

Next, he was told he must take both a written and a practical test, however, if he paid another 500 *baht*, they would overlook the practical test because it was obvious he had been driving for many years already.

"No problem," thought Riley. "I'd only end up punching the testing officer out anyway."

At this point I did not have the heart to interrupt him to tell him that practical tests were not mandatory and the staff had just earned themselves a little bonus.

He still had to undergo the written exam so was taken into a room and handed a piece of paper with twenty multiple-choice questions in English. He sat down with his pen and began to read the questionnaire. He was quick to notice that, for each question, one of the answer boxes was already ticked in pencil. It did not take Einstein to work out he had been given the answers. He went through the twenty questions simply writing over the pencil marks with his pen and handed the completed form to the lady.

She went away but came back in five minutes with the good news.
"You pass," she said.
"Eighteen from twenty".
"Hold on," replied Riley. "I marked the boxes with the pencil ticks.
Why did I only get eighteen right?"
"Always make two wrong. *Fa-lung* never get twenty."

Riley is an Englishman, fifty years old. He lives in a modest one-bedroom apartment in South Pattaya and has no real claims to fame. If he did have a framed letter on his wall, it would probably state; "Her Majesty's Government of the United Kingdom of Great Britain and Northern Ireland requests your presence elsewhere."

When I first met him a year ago, he had already been in Thailand for twelve years. He now runs a bar in a long-forgotten *soi*. The first thing that strikes any newcomer when visiting his bar is the *mamasan*. A woman in her late-thirties, she is tall by Thai standards, very solid and very sour. She is grossly unattractive and as mean as a junkyard dog.

Riley told me he only hired her because she works cheap but I think there was more to it than that. It was rumoured that she once worked as a bouncer at a very seedy Go Go Bar catering to the bottom end of the food chain. It was further rumoured that she had to leave after beating two customers to death using only her left breast. Their bodies could only be identified through dental records. Their 'crime', apparently, was they refused to buy her a 'lady drink'. Riley confessed that he gets away with only paying her 3,000 *baht* a month but she makes more than 10,000 *baht* in lady drinks. He swore it was purely a business relationship but from some of the looks she was giving him, I think he grants her a sexual favour from time to time - whenever she wants it.

One evening I caught up with Riley sitting on his usual stool in a corner of his bar and looking extremely forlorn. It was a sign to approach with caution.
"I'm scared," he whispered.
Thinking he had started seeing large purple spiders again, I tried to think of a polite way to suggest a couple more weeks in rehab.

"I'm a dragon," he continued.

This time he had really lost the plot.

"Oh, mate, you're no oil painting but I would not describe you as a dragon."

He cut me off. "Not just a dragon, but a golden dragon."

I started to back away a little, noting that Riley may need a little extra personal space. I know I certainly did. Once upon a time I knew a guy, coincidentally in a bar, who, as soon as he had a few under his belt, thought he was Janis Joplin. Consequently, I have had some experience with delusional people. He did do a good rendition of 'Me and Bobbie McGee' though. My earlier friend, not Riley.

"Is that good?" I asked softly.

"I don't know," came the slow and even softer response.

At this point I swear I heard the theme from *The X Files* and fully expected Mulder and Scully to walk up behind me and tap me on the shoulder.

"I just don't get it. I mean, why me? Hey! I drink like a fish, swear like a sailor, run a bar and a brothel for God's sake. I'm more like a bunyip than a dragon."

For the uninitiated, a bunyip is a mythical creature that inhabits the wilds of Australia. It is a rather innocuous and benign character whose only real claim to fame is that it seems to cop the blame when anything goes wrong.

"Sweetheart, who drank my bottle of 16-year-old scotch?"

"The bunyip did it."

A dragon is also a mythical creature but generally not so benign. There are, of course, good dragons as well as bad dragons, but mostly they just breathe fire and scare the living shit out of people.

"Darling, who toasted Grandma?"

"The dragon got her."

It would be difficult for a rational person to confuse these two legendary creatures. One is so regal, so fearsome, so God-like, while the other is well, nobody really knows what it looks like. Just as it would be difficult to confuse my friend Riley with say, a king, a president or a high priest.

It all began with a dream, he said. Let's face it, most absurdities do. His *mamasan* dreamt a dragon was chasing her but she could not escape fast enough. Her legs were heavy and she was moving in slow motion. When it got close to her, she turned and saw that the dragon's face was that of Riley and she knew then, it would not hurt her. Thais put a lot of importance in dreams, so the next day she visited a spiritualist slash palm-reader slash quack. The lady confirmed that what *mamasan* saw was a good dragon, a golden dragon, and it was a good sign and would not harm her. She said her boss, Riley, may have been a dragon in a previous life and now, in this life, he was very special, very important and very good luck to have around.

This begged the obvious question
"If you are so high and mighty, what are the perks? Surely they must have to sacrifice a virgin to you each month or so."
"I wish! But since she had that dream, she has made my life hell. She's worse than a mother hen. She wants me to cut down on drinking, she won't let me smoke, she watches what I eat and sometimes she follows me around. She believes she has to protect me from danger. She's like my own personal bodyguard."

I had always assumed that dragons could pretty much take care of themselves but, if one ever needed a bodyguard, she certainly had the physique for it. And apparently, the experience.
"You complain too much," I said. "It could be worse."
"Yeah, I suppose so. Hey, she's gone to the loo. Give me a drag on your cigarette, will ya?"

Riley is an Australian, forty-six years old. We have been friends ever since we started university together way back in the seventies. We did not finish our respective courses at the same time because, although he was academically minded, I was alcoholically minded. He finished his course a year before me. Our paths then took different turns but we still remained in contact.

His career went completely off the rails when he decided he wanted to be a priest. Incredulous as it seemed to me and in spite of my attempts at talking him out of it, he stuck to his guns. I told him I thought that, to become a priest, you must first believe in God. He explained that, although desirable, it did not appear to be a prerequisite. So, off he went to priest school or whatever it is called.

Needless to say, I was not surprised when six months later he told me he had left. In fact, he had been asked to leave when, one morning during prayers or vespers, he stood up and proclaimed, "I need a fuck!" His official letter of eviction cited that he had emitted an "audible obscenity". Obviously he need not bother taking up professional tennis. The letter went on to say that he had also been indulging in "chronic self-abuse". It seemed they had never seen anyone who could slap the monkey as much as he could. He even went to the doctor after his member became red raw. The doctor prescribed some ointment to rub on the affected region and all was well until his bosses discovered he was going through two bottles of the stuff a day. It appeared he had not been cured.

He next settled for the safety and security of a steady mundane job while I tried my hand at many different occupations. The result was that he managed to save some money whereas I discovered a lot of things I am not good at. Eventually Riley came to the conclusion that he had worn out his welcome back home so decided to head for places unknown and adventures unfathomed. If he had an official letter from the Australian Government, it would probably read: "The Prime Minister of the Commonwealth of Australia wants you to fuck off."

He thought about trying his hand in Asia where at least he would be a complete unknown entity to the unsuspecting population. He guessed it might take a few years before they discovered he was an habitual underachiever who was of no benefit to anyone. And where else do habitual underachiever running away from home go? Just as I did some years before, he found himself in Pattaya. Here, in the potpourri of expats, sexpats, dropouts, dropkicks, misfits, miscreants, government agents and draft-dodgers, he feels right at home.

Riley is a Canadian, fifty-three years old. Like most Canadians living outside their country, he spends most of his day telling people, "I am not an American." It seems Canadians are often confused with Americans and, with no disrespect to their close neighbours, don't appreciate it.

"But you sure talk like a Yank," I would goad him.

"I am not a Yank. I'm Canadian. There's a difference."
I could always tell when my little joke went too far because he would start calling me a Kiwi. Australians, with total disrespect to their neighbours across the Tasman Sea, don't like being called New Zealanders. At that point, he knew he had won and I would change the subject.

He manages a small indoor beer bar in Central Pattaya where, every day, he can be found sitting near the corner on his favourite bar stool. Beside him, wedged firmly into the corner, stands his pride and joy - and possibly his best friend - a tall, leafy, green tree sprouting from an earthenware pot.

Riley is a vodka man. He used to drink beer but noticed he was putting on too much weight so, a year ago, switched over to vodka. Vodka-tonic, vodka-ice or vodka-water. I noticed that, each time he finished a glass, he would empty the remaining ice-cubes and dregs of the vodka into the pot containing his pet tree. The last time I saw him do this, he bragged about owning the only tree in the world that thrived on vodka. To prove his point, he got up from the bar stool and stood toe-to-toe beside it.

"When I bought it just over eight months ago, it was this tall," he said, positioning his hand a few inches above his head.

"I water it every morning and feed it vodka all night. Look at it! It must be eight feet tall. It's grown two feet in eight months! Call the Guinness Book of Records!"

This was very impressive so I went to get a closer look at the alcoholic tree. Yes, it was at least eight feet tall. Yes, it looked in excellent health with barely a mark to be found on the bright green foliage. But before returning to my seat, I noticed something else.

"Mate, don't bother calling Guinness. You'd be better to give Ripley's Believe It or Not a call. Tell them you own the only plastic tree in the world that grows when you feed it vodka!"

"What the fuck are you talking about?"

"Mate, the tree is plastic. It is fake. Imitation. Not alive."

"Bullshit!" Riley moved in for a closer look at his tree. The moment he bit into one of the leaves, his face said it all. Returning to his seat, he looked like a kid who just found out there was no Santa Claus.

"Well, how come it has grown two feet?" Defiant to the last.

"Mate, it hasn't grown. You've shrunk!"

So here we all are. It is said that water finds its own level or, more to the point, everyone rises or sinks to his own level of incompetence. In Pattaya, my friends and I fit in to the burgeoning population of foreign potential deportees like we were born to it. Here, whether we are waiting out or hiding out, we are all kindred spirits and living the life of Riley.

34

Breaking Up is Hard to Do

Recently, on one of my evening research missions, I was introduced to some guys at the bar and invited to join their conversation. The discussion covered the three main topics of expat conversation – Thailand, Thai people and Thai girlfriends. The anecdotes and laughter were running thick when one of the group posed a challenging question. "How do you get rid of one? I've been in an on-off relationship for three years," he continued. "And I'm sick of it and sick of her. She's left me before but she keeps coming back! No matter what I do, she just won't leave for good."

Sitting beside him to his left, was a beautiful Thai lady. I only really noticed her because she was gorgeous and possessed magnificent breasts. He put his arm around her occasionally and had obviously paid for her orange juice. I thought to myself, hell, if he wants to get rid of her then I wouldn't mind being around to catch his discard. But no, I have had girlfriends before, not only Thai, who are pains in the arse to live with but in public, come over so sweet and adorable that your friends are green with envy.

As it turned out, she was not the girlfriend he wanted to break up with. She was one of the reasons he wanted to get rid of the current incumbent. So the bar conversation then turned to focus on the problem of getting rid of a girlfriend. This was particularly amusing because, looking at the five of us, there would be little chance any of us could attract a female of our own species back in our own countries. We were not what you would call the pick of the litter. Old, fat and ugly, or to be politically correct, mature, jolly and facially-challenged.

But that was why we were all in Pattaya in the first place and where, now, we were faced with a hitherto unthinkable dilemma – how to tactfully, politely and amicably end a relationship. Far be it from me to enter into such a sexist conversation, but I did.

The first suggestion was more of an admission of defeat. "It's impossible. They just won't go!" Thanks for that. My suggestion soon followed. "I don't know the answer but, if I ever discover a sure-fire method, I'll keep it secret. Then I'll publish an information booklet and sell it for five hundred *baht* per copy." Mercenary as always.

The brainstorming continued with the next suggestion, accompanied by laughter, being the standard joke among the male expat community. "The quickest way to get rid of your girlfriend is to tell her you are broke." The general consensus from the discussion that followed was, although it should work in principle, it was not always the unfailing solution it was cracked up to be.

In my own case, I told my current girlfriend right from the beginning of our relationship that I did not have a lot of money. I remind her of it every day but she still stays with me. What I have determined from some of her conversation is that she doesn't believe me. She thinks I am only saying that to test her – to see if she loves me for myself or the money she thinks I have. "You *fa-lung*. All *fa-lung* have big money."

It appears the bar girls of Pattaya are under the mistaken belief that all foreigners are rich. And who can blame them? Every day they see foreign men staying in expensive hotels, eating at fine restaurants and spending money like drunken sailors. And if we weren't rich, we could not have afforded the airfare to Thailand in the first place. They don't realize that many of those free-spending holidaymakers have been saving up for a year in order to behave extravagantly for a week or two.

184

"I tried that too," he said. "But she still would not leave."

A story was then recounted about a *fa-lung* who became so desperate he gave the girl 10,000 *baht* to leave. All went well, she accepted the money, packed all her things and left. Two weeks later she was back. "I love you and miss you too much." Being the kind-hearted guy he was, he let her stay. Plan B was a complete failure and he was back to square one. Of course she came back. She knew he was a soft touch so, once the money was spent, she came back for more.

We then looked at the problem from another perspective. On the occasion that a bar girl wants to break up with her *fa-lung*, what does she do? If she has found herself a better (i.e. richer) *fa-lung*, she moves in with him. If not, she simply walks out, finds another bar to work in and maybe even changes room. If the besotted boyfriend tries to find her, the 'Cone of Silence' descends over her friends and he is left with a needle-in-a-haystack search. Eventually he either gives up or returns home.

The problem with a foreigner adopting these same tactics is that he may own the condo in which he is living or have a long-term lease. Even if he is staying in temporary accommodation and is able to move to another hotel or apartment the next day, the Thai grapevine in Pattaya is the most efficient communication system in the modern world. Even if he was staying in Central Pattaya and moves to *Naklua* or *Jomtien* in order to avoid contact with his ex-girlfriend, all that is required is that he visit a bar where one of her friends is working and the friend can make a phone call. If he returns to his favourite watering-hole, one of the girls at that bar can make a phone call. Five minutes later his 'ex' may be standing by his side. Don't laugh – this actually happens. Since living in hiding does not sound very appealing, Plan C received no votes of approval.

We were left with the sad and sorry truth that you have to be cruel to be kind. The break-up has to be quick, as amicable as possible and leave the aggrieved partner with no doubt it is final. Everything of hers must be removed from his apartment, including her toothbrush. If he cannot or does not wish to change accommodation, he should change the door locks and ensure the people at reception were informed they are no longer a couple. No further correspondence should be entered into. No more money should be forthcoming and definitely no, "Ok, you can stay for just one more night." This plan received a general vote of agreement.

The major problem with Plan D is you need to have a heart of stone in order to carry it out effectively. Soon after all agreeing it was the best strategy we could come up with, the dominos started to fall.

"Yeah, I know, but she has been a real darling and I could not do that to her."

"Me too. Mine has not done anything really bad. I'm the one who's been the 'butterfly'. I'd feel too guilty."

"All she would have to do would be start crying and I'd give in."

There's the rub. We could have sat there drinking for the rest of the night and come up with all the strategies and schemes known to man, but not one of us had the balls to carry them out. We were a bunch of wimps with spines of foam rubber. This begged the final question about who holds the power. Is it the old, experienced, well-educated, man-of-the-world with the money to do whatever he likes whenever he likes, or is it the young Thai girl with the cute figure from the poor village who looks up at him and, with sad, brown eyes, whispers, "I love you too much"? The jury took a full three seconds to return a unanimous verdict whereupon we moved the discussion to the easier subject of how to solve the problem of global warming.

35

Sanook Soup

Ingredients:

three days with nothing to do.
six to twelve Pattaya bar girls.
up to five *fa-lung* friends.
a dozen large bottles of Sangthip whisky.
two dozen large bottles of Coke.
enough cold beer for three days – minimum of
24 bottles per person per day.
enough vehicles to fit all the above.
ear plugs.
tapes of your favourite *fa-lung* music.
towel, change of clothes, toiletries etc.
lots of money.

Method:

I wrote in 'Buffalo River' that I would go back to *Kanchanaburi* one day, but in my wildest dreams I could never have imagined the circumstances that would lead to my return visit, nor could I have imagined the course of entertainment I would be force-fed. John Lennon once sang that "life is what happens to you while you're busy making other plans." (Not original but I like John Lennon so will give him the credit for now.)

It began innocently enough, with a visit to my then favourite bar. After ordering my first beer, I noticed a lot of conversation and excitement among the girls. It wasn't very long before one approached me and asked if I had ever been to *Kanchanaburi* before. I replied in the affirmative stating that I wanted to go again because I did not get to see much of the place the last time.

She translated what I had said to one of the other girls who then passed the information along to the rest of the troupe. One of the girls then explained that the bar would be closed the following day because they were all going on a trip to *Kanchanaburi*.
"What, all of you?"
"Yes. *Mamasan* hire car. We go twelve o'clock."
Before I could wish them, "Have a good trip," the *mamasan*, who had been busy talking on her mobile phone, came over to speak with me.
"We close tomorrow. Go *Kanchanaburi*."
"So I heard."
"You want come?"

I was confused and with only half a Carlsberg in my system, my sober mind was not fully prepared. Why did she want me to come along?
"Is there enough room?" I asked.
"Sure. Have two minibus. No poblem."
Why would a dozen Bar girls, the *mamasan* and two Thai drivers want a *fa-lung* to come with them for a day out? Because they enjoyed my company? Not likely. The cynical answer came to me. Money. *Fa-lung* are allowed to attend what should be exclusively Thai affairs for one reason only – they are the ATM machine.

I wanted to thank the *mamasan* for the invitation but respectfully decline due to a prior commitment. She must have heard my brain ticking over.
"You no pay. Everything free! I pay. No poblem."
Her response threw me off guard and, whether triggered by the word 'free' or by a desire to do something I had never experienced before, I heard myself saying "Ok."

Arrangements were made to pick me up the following day at noon. That night I did not get much sleep because I was worried about what scam, if any, they were trying to pull on this stupid *fa-lung*. Nevertheless, the following day at noon, I was waiting at Foodland. I had an overnight bag containing one change of clothing in case we went swimming. I did have 4,000 *baht* on me but no ATM card. I reasoned, if it was a con, that was all the money they were going to get from me.

At 12:45pm, a minibus full of excited girls stopped in the carpark. *Mamasan* was sitting in the front passenger seat and gave instructions to the driver as she handed him a wad of money. Three girls followed the driver into Foodland while the rest of them stored my bag and made room for me in the back of the bus. Some reshuffling was required because, squeezed behind the two front seats were two large plastic garbage bins. With no leg room there, I was directed to sit in the seat behind and two of the girls moved forward. This was very thoughtful because they understood a *fa-lung* needed to stretch his legs whereas a Thai girl could sit cross-legged all day and not get cramps.

The driver and his entourage reappeared with two shopping trolleys overloaded with goodies which I noticed were mostly alcoholic. Cartons of Heineken, Singha and Carlsberg plus a carton of Sangthip. As if an afterthought, there were two cartons of large bottles of Coke. The other trolley was filled with bags of ice. Wow, this *mamasan* sure knew how to travel! Everyone enthusiastically helped unload the bottles into the garbage bins and empty the ice over each layer.

While this was going on, the other van parked along side. *Mamasan* handed over some more loot and the procedure was repeated for the second batch of party-goers. It was difficult not to get wrapped up in the party atmosphere but I kept checking my watch as the time ticked by. If we were indeed going to *Kanchanaburi*, we would not get back to Pattaya before the early hours of the morning. I wished I had asked a few more questions before agreeing to come along.

So we set off - eleven bar girls, one *mamasan*, two drivers and me. The rear door of my van had no sooner slammed shut than drinks were called for all round. Most of the girls preferred to drink Heineken so it was obvious the Carlsberg had been ordered for me. The bottles were passed over the back for opening and then distributed to the happy campers, including one for the driver. After my third bottle, I learned that, in all the excitement, they had forgotten one important element – a bottle opener. The beer I was passing behind me for opening was being opened by an improvised human bottle opener - one girl with the skill to open bottles with her teeth. I watched as the dentist's dream deftly removed the cap from my Carlsberg in one swift movement.

"No poblem," she smiled.

The journey to *Kanchanaburi* took seven hours with numerous comfort stops to relieve swollen Thai bladders. Along the way I learned the plan was to spend the night and return to Pattaya the next afternoon. I wish they had told me before as I had brought no shaving gear, toothbrush or towel. I wondered where we were all going to sleep but the *mamasan* looked as if she knew what she was doing.

Upon arrival, we stopped to ask directions. I then found out none of them had ever been to *Kanchanaburi* before. So much for the *mamasan* knowing what she was doing.. A few back streets later and we were at the river. I helped the girls unpack and carry everything to a wooden platform by the water's edge. There did not appear to be any hotels nearby. *Mamasan* returned with a Thai man who directed us to move the gear onto a large floating platform. It turned out to be a barge or houseboat and was the reason we had come to *Kanchanaburi*.

The wooden vessel was rectangular in shape and at a guess about eight metres wide by twelve metres long. Both the covered upper deck and the lower one were surrounded by a waist-high wooden railing. At one end was a small toilet, a storage area and a kitchen. At the other end was another storage area plus a mini sound studio filled with a vast collection of CDs and tapes, a lot of CD players, tape decks and amplifiers with lots of knobs, buttons and switches. The ceiling was decorated with a galaxy of multicoloured disco lighting and the whole area was surrounded by six large speakers, the largest two being at least two metres high and a metre wide.

I took on the responsibility of filling two large ice boxes with what remained of the beer. Two girls were sent out for more ice, more cartons of beer arrived, mats were rolled out over the floor and food started appearing. The scene was energetic, with everyone except for the stupid *fa-lung* knowing what they were doing.

It wasn't long before the platoon of extra helpers left the boat, the mooring ropes were detached and we were moving. A small boat with an inboard engine manoeuvred us into mid-river and then towed us at a nice even clip. I noticed hundreds of other similar barges moored to the banks. We sat around the mat and consumed a sumptuous meal. By now we were all above the legal driving limit and most were above the legal walking limit. Nevertheless the meal was delicious and washed down with cold beer from the seemingly bottomless ice boxes.

Once the plates and what remained of the food was cleared away, the mats were rolled up and stored. Just as I scanned the dark featureless riverbank in search of lights which may indicate a hotel, an explosion, sounding as if World War Three had just broken out, interrupted my concentration. The vessel shook with powerful vibration as my ears shuddered under the weight of decibels of noise being forcibly rammed into my head. I turned to see the source of the incredible din. It came from the mountain of speakers at the front and the fuse was lit by a smiling Thai DJ as he adjusted the volume – upwards.

The girls screamed and began to dance wildly to the incredible noise that must have been one of their favourite Thai disco tunes. By this stage I was very tired and emotional and looking forward to a comfortable night's sleep in a nice hotel room. But the floating disco continued. I was dragged kicking and screaming onto the dance floor but my protests went unheeded because they all thought I was demonstrating some weird new Western dance steps.

After cruising for about two hours the pilot steered toward the bank. With a skill showing he had performed the manoeuvre many times before, the barge was pressed up against a not too stable jetty. The darkness of the surrounds led me to believe the hotel was either going through a blackout or, my greatest fear, was nonexistence. It did not matter to the drunken revellers as they continued to dance to the pounding, thumping, tuneless rhythm. And it continued all night.

That big, hot, round thing in the sky worked its way above the eastern horizon just as the first females collapsed into a coma. My eardrums barely noticed the DJ had switched off the jet engine blasters. The mats were rolled out again and carry-bags placed for pillows. The troupe laid themselves out on the mats like a can of sardines and I was directed to join them. There was not going to be a hotel but with my ears still ringing, my eyes stinging and my head spinning, I accepted the wooden floor with gratitude.

I was asleep a full three minutes when *mamasan* decided we should get the show on the road. My cursing and complaining was ignored and I was told we could shower at the limited camping facilities set up on the shore. There was a concrete shower block of six cubicles opposite a toilet block of the same number, a bamboo hut that sold toiletries and some tables and chairs which substituted for a restaurant. I made it up the incline and purchased soap, shampoo, disposable razor, toothbrush and toothpaste. There were no towels so I used my clothes to dry myself before putting on the spare set I had brought. The water was freezing but at this point in time, I didn't care.

Back on the boat, some very tired and very quiet young ladies were laying out food. As we sat to eat, the roar of the engine from our towing craft signalled that we were, once again, on our way. The trip back took three hours because we stopped at sights of significance along route. The first was a cemetery for some of the POWs who died here during World War II. The second was a *Wat* which meant a little more to the Thais than some old graveyard filled with dead *fa-lung*.

We docked back in *Kanchanaburi* where I recovered sufficiently to start packing up our gear to hasten our getaway. No one else was bothering so I asked one of the girls what the plan was. She joyfully replied that *mamasan* was not happy with only one night so had decided that we should stay for one more night. I couldn't believe it. We were only stopping to stock up on supplies and were going back out on the floating disco.

Leaving our gear on the boat, we piled into the two vans and drove into the town proper to do some shopping. But first we had to stop for lunch. A restaurant was chosen and we occupied several of the wooden tables. The meal consumed, I saw *mamasan* looking a little apprehensive as she ratted around in her handbag. Before I could make a hasty retreat, the driver approached and beckoned me towards him and the *mamasan*.
"I not have enough money until go to ATM. I can borrow money?" she asked me.
Here we go! I knew it, expected it, so why was I so shocked to hear it now.
"How much do you need?"
"You have four thousand?"

She must have gone through my pockets while I was asleep. How else did she know I had exactly four thousand *baht* on me? I handed over the money taking one last long look at the four crisp notes I was sure I would never see again. She thanked me and assured me she would return it once she went to an ATM. She then paid the restaurant bill and disappeared with a driver and one of the vans leaving the girls and I to do some window shopping.

Realistically, there was no need for me to complain. If the trip cost me four thousand *baht* then I was sure getting value for money. The transport, the boat trip, the beer and the food I consumed would have cost far more than that. Now we were staying for another night, I was not so concerned about the money.

About an hour later, the van returned and you could have knocked me over with a feather when the first thing *mamasan* did was walk straight over to me and hand me back four thousand *baht*. Overcome with guilt, I felt like a low-life, freeloading, ungrateful rat - to put it mildly. I decided I would show my appreciation (and clear my conscience) by paying for the next meal and anything else necessary until all the money was spent.

Back on the boat, the beer and food stocks had been replenished so it was just a matter of climbing on board and casting off. My problem now was that I was wearing the only spare set of clothing I had brought along. Yesterday's attire was, shall we say, on the nose and I had forgotten to buy another set while we were ashore. I couldn't have anyway, since *mamasan* borrowed all the money I had. One of the girls came to my rescue and told me she would wash them for me. They would dry quickly and would be wearable tomorrow. What an angel.

The second night on the floating disco was similar to the first, with one exception. The partying and the music stopped before 2:00am and not at sunrise. For this, my ears and I were extremely grateful. The DJ captain woke us at around eleven so we could use the shore facilities and eat before cruising back into the town. *Mamasan* appeared satisfied with the second night and content to bring the two-day party to a close.

The trip back to Pattaya was truly boring with most of us sleeping all the way. The heavy drinking session of the forward journey was not attempted. Our one stop for a meal gave me some satisfaction as I gladly parted with just over a thousand *baht* to pay the bill. What price a conscience?

So now I have been to *Kanchanaburi* twice and basically seen nothing. I'll stick with looking at the pictures in the travel brochures from now on. Twice is enough.

36

The Toothbrush Conspiracy

It was while researching case studies for 'The Butterfly Myth' that things got interesting. Just when I was becoming disillusioned with the Quixotic quest to uncover a true Pattaya Butterfly, I stumbled upon an even more interesting story. I decided to take a different approach and, instead of searching for a strategy as to how to become a Butterfly, I analysed the reason that many seemed to fail in the attempt. Conspiracy theorists of the world hold on to your paranoia, because I have uncovered the most insidious and potentially, the most costly conspiracy of them all. It centres around the humble toothbrush and every wanna-be Butterfly should take heed.

Let's face it, relationships in Pattaya are not what you would call 'mainstream'. Instead of beginning with a smile, a twinkle in the eye, flowers, chocolates then a movie or two, romance Pattaya-style starts with a smile, a twinkle in the eye, a bar fine, then sex. The flowers, chocolates and movies are just time and money wasters. It follows then that relationships are incredibly easy to get into, require very little effort and a very short time.

The problem for foreign men is these relationships can be very difficult to get out of. It stems from the principle of supply and demand. There is an oversupply of willing ladies in Pattaya and an undersupply of foreign men. Although both physical appearance and age count for absolutely nothing, there is an even shorter supply of generous, kind and 'nice' foreign men. Consequently, once a bar girl thinks she has caught one, she is loath to give him up without a fight.

Most generous, kind and 'nice' foreign men, on the other hand, are usually only here on holiday. They want to have fun, want to sample more than one of Pattaya's delights and enjoy a degree of independence. They are the 'wanna-be' Butterflies and this is the dilemma.

From the man's point of view, once a bar girl spends the night with him, a Butterfly will allow her to leave early the next morning. Here's your money – don't call me, I'll call you. If the guy decides he likes her and that he enjoyed her company, he may bar fine her for the next night as well. This is not too damaging but the girl will be quick to pick up the signals. "He could have chosen to go with any one of a thousand other girls but he chose me again. He really likes me."

The trouble begins once he bar fines the same girl for the third consecutive night. Her suspicions that he really does like her have been confirmed and the prospects of a long-term commitment become very real to her. "He loves me." The signal is loud and clear and she is not going to let him go very easily. The plot thickens, as they say.

Enter the toothbrush. Many men mistakenly believe the bar girl's most lethal weapon is her mobile phone, but this is like comparing a bow and arrow with an Exocet missile – both can kill but the Exocet, or toothbrush, causes a lot more collateral damage.

When a bar girl first enters his hotel room, what does she do? She goes to the bathroom. And what, besides the obvious, does she do in there? She counts the toothbrushes. More than one and she knows he is already taken. She wants no arguments with another bar girl or a 'wife' fighting for his attention, so she may back off somewhat. If, however, she spots a solitary toothbrush standing in the glass, she deduces that this particular *fa-lung* may, as yet, be unclaimed. Providing he is a good man with a good heart, she can use her feminine charms to hold on to him for at least another night.

If successful, after the second or third night together, before she leaves, she will deliberately leave her toothbrush behind. This simple gesture has sinister ramifications. She has now marked her territory. His bathroom is now a 'two toothbrush' bathroom.

Research has revealed that the toothbrush weapon is most often used on the third morning but it can be called into play earlier, depending on how keen the lady is to go back to work in the bar.

But why a toothbrush? Why not a lipstick, nail polish or a hair brush? Because a toothbrush is a very personal item and it signifies a degree of permanence. A toothbrush indicates its owner lives there or at least, stays overnight. The toothbrush is the thin end of the wedge. Next will come some make-up, then a few items of clothing (to save her going back to her room each day to change), and shoes. Stealthily, she will slowly turn his room into her room, his apartment into her apartment.

So, for the guy who strives to keep his independence while sharing his wealth among more than one pretty face, there are two alternative bathroom strategies to employ. The first is to go to a supermarket, buy about a dozen toothbrushes of assorted shapes, sizes and colours, then fill the glass in the bathroom with them. Any new overnight guest, following her bathroom inspection, will assume he is either over the top with his dental hygiene or is the mother of all Butterflies (or a helicopter). With such stiff competition, she will hopefully conclude there are easier fish to fry in Pattaya.

The second is vigilance. In the morning, before she walks out the door, he should check the bathroom. If he finds a second toothbrush in the glass, he then hands it to her with the unambiguous message, "Don't forget your toothbrush!"

37

Football Fever

Well, it's over for another four years, that tournament that excites the living hell out of one half the population while boring the other half to tears. As Pattaya settles into a post-World Cup depression, I pause to reflect upon the events that excited much of the globe over the last month.

Fans from the Land of the Great Unwashed call it 'football' as opposed to Rugby. Australians and Americans call it 'soccer' to differentiate between each country's football codes and the round-ball game. For the sake of this story, I will refer to it as 'soccer'.

If you were in Pattaya for June of 2002 and happened to be one of the few people disinterested in soccer, the best thing you could have done was to seek out an Australian to talk to. For as sport-loving as Australians are, if we're not in it, we don't give a rat's arse about it. As long as New Zealand don't win.

Incidentally, why weren't we in it? Australians fought and won two world wars almost single-handedly after defeating the might of the British Empire with an ill-equipped band of ex-convict gold miners at the famous Battle of The Eureka Stockade (the history books are wrong), and yet we were not included in the World Cup? Is that fair? Of course it's not, but I'm getting off the track so back to Pattaya.

The forest of green was deathly silent except for the occasional sound of a tear splashing on a beer mat. I was in an Irish bar and felt totally isolated as we watched the Germany v Ireland game. At some point, in what seemed to be the first six hours of running backwards and forwards, Germany scored a goal. The game was now drawing to a close and, at one-nil down, all was not looking good for the Paddys.

Suddenly I was awakened as the bar erupted in screaming, cheering, jumping up and down, high-five-ing, back slapping and beer toasting. One of the Irish players, who I am sure will soon be Knighted, kicked the round ball into the big rectangular net. The hooting and hollering continued during the innumerable replays of that magical moment and did not stop until well after full-time had sounded. Again and again we watched the player performing somersaults, handstands and thumping his chest before being set upon by his team mates for some hugging, kissing and, I'm only guessing here, some simulated sex. Even I was caught up in the euphoria when beers were purchased for the Neanderthal Australian who did not have a clue as to the significance of this momentous occasion.

But wait a minute, the result of the match was a one-all draw. If this is how excited they get when their team draws, I dread to think what the commotion would have been like if the Paddys had actually *won* the match. Back in Ireland, they probably would have partied well into the next week and, dare I say it, nine months later the country would have another baby boom.

This got me thinking about the fanaticism that grips supporters every time a game of soccer is played. It looks such a timid game that the adrenaline overload among devotees appears out of place. Not that it doesn't require a lot of skill and athleticism to play, it just seems to take more courage to watch it.

For some weeks prior to the start of the competition, press reports the world over focused on the negative aspects of soccer. The word 'hooligan' was mentioned many times as well as the international efforts to stop unsavoury types from entering Japan or Korea. Apart from one notorious bar in Pattaya that profited very nicely from the international attention it was getting, the fans here were generally well behaved.

Australians are an opinionated bunch. We could solve all the world's problems if only the world would listen to us. The next Global Summit should be held in any Aussie pub on a Friday afternoon. There, the world's power brokers could hear genuine, practical solutions to their problems. In that respect, I have a theory about soccer violence and hooliganism. I believe there is so much violence off the field because there is so little violence on the field.

To an outsider it appears that the game was invented so mothers the world over could gleefully send little Johnny or Paolo off to his soccer match and remain comforted by the knowledge that he would return to her bosom in an uninjured state.

"Mummy, can I go out and play soccer today?"

"Sure, darling, go out and have fun."

Compare this to her fears should he only wish to sit in the crowd.

"Mummy, can I go out and watch Billy play soccer for the under-eight's today?"

"Certainly not! You know how dangerous it is!"

Two thousand years ago in Rome, the crowds at the Colosseum were the best behaved in recorded history. There was no jostling for seats, no fights in the stands, no need for Centurion Crowd Controllers to segregate the Lion supporters from the Christian supporters and no turning over and burning chariots after the games just because your favourite gladiator got the chop. All the blood-letting was in the arena and the crowd was satisfied. Their appetite for violence was fed.

Australians have rugby league and rugby union. The purpose of these games is to injure or maim as many of the opposing team as possible. Win by attrition. Last man standing. It is very exciting to watch two men, each 110 kilograms plus, smashing into each other at full pace. This is followed by a momentary hush in the crowd as we wait to see which of them, if either, get up. Some men have been known to play forty minutes of rugby with a broken arm. Their dedication, or stupidity, is such that they refuse to feel the pain or leave the field of play. Before it became a legal requirement that any player found to be bleeding must leave the field, I witnessed a man wiping blood away from his eyes in order to see out the rest of the match. The next day, newspapers reported he had to go to hospital and have fourteen stitches to the wound in his head. These are men.

We also have Australian Rules which, although not designed to be a contact sport, has its share of violence. Americans have their own brand of brutality and again, crowd violence is limited or nonexistent because of it. These big men, made to look even bigger by the six inches of padding wrapped around every part of their body, deliberately go on to the field with the intention of hurting the opposition. Bone crunching stuff.

The second reason for the off-field violence exhibited by soccer supporters surely must be the scoring system. A miserable one point for a goal is just not enough! In a game where it is apparently so difficult to get the ball into the net, surely it should be worth more. Both codes of rugby commonly achieve scores in the twenties and thirties, as does the American game. Aussie Rules often has scores up around the hundred mark. These games are exciting to watch, especially if your team wins.

Another reason must be the propensity of drawn matches in soccer. I have to confess that to sit through ninety minutes of to-ing and fro-ing only to have the game end in a nil-all draw makes me want to hit or destroy something too. In other codes of football, draws are very rare and nil-all draws are almost unheard of. The crowd get what they want – lots of violence, lots of points scored and, most importantly, a result.

Or – it could be the size of the ball has a lot to do with it. I know this is a radical theory but, have you noticed in ball sports, the bigger the ball, the bigger the problems are with the crowd?

Consider golf. The game is played using a very small ball and yet there has never been a riot amongst a golfing audience, has there?

202

Tennis? Same thing – small balls. Not once have the police been called in with water cannon to settle the Wimbledon crowd. Although tennis and golf are not what you would call team sports, nevertheless I believe they deserve to be included for the sake of comparison.

"What about cricket?" I hear you ask. Surely that has got to be one of the world's most boring sports? Very few injuries, almost zero physical contact. Why isn't there crowd violence and hooliganism associated with that sport? That is a good point and I'm glad you brought it up.

My theory is that cricket spectators are too busy sleeping to worry about starting fights. Remember too that cricket has a lot of scoring. Test match results in the order of six for 320 or seven for 400 are commonplace. The snoring crowd is impressed by big numbers. I admit drawn games or series are too common for my liking, but I'm sure, with slight rule changes, this eventuality could be removed.

Sport	Ball Size	Scoring	Drawn Games	On-field Violence	Crowd Behaviour
Golf	Really tiny	High	Never	Very Rare	Standing and tired
Tennis	Small	Medium	Never	Very Rare	Controlled and snooty
Cricket	Small	High	Rare	Never	Asleep
Lawn Bowls	Small to medium	Low	Never	Very Rare	Under medication
Rugby	Medium	High	Rare	Often	Vocal, enthusiastic, non-violent
American Football	Medium	High	Rare	Often	Vocal, enthusiastic, non-violent
Soccer	Big	Low	Frequent	Very Rare	Vocal, violent, hooligans
Basketball	Really big	High	Rare	Rare	Vocal, enthusiastic, non-violent

Football Fever   A Fool In Paradise

To make it easier, I have constructed a table to compare important characteristics of some popular ball sports. Even though I could further illustrate my point with a series of graphs and pie charts, I think you will agree this enlightening table proves my theories beyond any reasonable doubt.

Not being one to criticize anything without offering an alternative, I have some suggestions to the governing body of world soccer to liven the game up. I'll leave them to work out the finer points of this new football order, but I believe it should be made a full-contact sport with defending players allowed to get the ball away from the opposition any way they like. This would give the crowd the violence they have been craving. No longer would a player have to give an Oscar-winning performance of severe injury each time he trips over his own shoelaces. Now, when he is tackled and goes down in a screaming heap, the pain will be real.

Next, get rid of the goalkeeper. Why should he be the only player on the field who can touch the ball with his hands? These guys stop the game scores reaching a level to get excited about. His job is a thankless one anyway. If his team loses, he usually gets the blame. If his team wins, the credit goes to the prima donna who scored the winning goal.

Next, the scoring system. Make any goal scored from a kick in play worth ten points, off the head, eight points and any other legal part of the body, six points. An own goal or one scored from a penalty kick should be worth five points.

Finally, reduce the size of the ball down to the same size as a lawn bowl. This will not necessarily make the game more exciting to play or watch but, as I have already shown, it will have a psychological effect on the crowd. According to a complex mathematical formula I myself devised, this will have the equivalent effect of administering half a valium to each spectator.

It would be unrealistic to expect all of these innovations to be introduced overnight. They should be phased in gradually, to give the players and spectators alike the chance to warm to the fresh, more exciting game. Sure, mothers could no longer send their little boys or girls out to play the 'safe' game, but the paying public in the grandstands, those who relish off-field violence, may now find their talents could be more useful on the field.

38

Dear Mum

Abelated Merry Christmas and Happy New Year. I'm sorry it
has been so long since I have written but I have been quite busy
here in Thailand. I hope they are taking good care of you in the
Harmony Bay Retirement Home. Thank you for the $10 you sent me
for my birthday. It came in very handy and, in fact, I used it to pay a
fine. Don't worry, it was nothing serious, just one of those petty fines
one incurs over here in Pattaya. By the way, I am forty-five, not thirty-
two.

Good news! I now have a girlfriend and I'm sure you would really
like her. Her name is *Lek*, she is twenty-six years old and we hit it off
from the very first time we saw each other. I know you have heard bad
stories about Thai girls, Mum, but *Lek* is different. We met in a local
pub where she worked as the cashier. She had only been working there
for one week. She is smart, very pretty, but also very shy. She speaks
good English and some German. She has been to Germany and Denmark
on holiday and also worked in a Karaoke restaurant in Singapore for
six months.

Before coming to Pattaya she was employed in a clothing factory in
Bangkok where she worked long hours, seven days a week and for not
much money. Now that her mother is very sick and needs an operation,
Lek decided to find work here in Pattaya to help her family out.

Lek comes from a small village in a place called *Korat*. She invited me home recently to meet her parents. When we arrived, they all came out to meet me – her mother, father, four brothers and a small baby the family is taking care of. *Lek* calls her 'Luke' which is a strange name for a girl. Her family was very friendly and smiled all the time. They all seemed very happy to meet me and have even given me a Thai name – *Kwai. Lek* said it means 'happy person'.

They certainly enjoyed all the presents we brought for them, especially the television set. It cost me a bit of money and I was worried about taking it on the bus but *Lek* explained that it was Thai tradition for a visitor to bring gifts and it will keep me in good stead with her family. Family values are really important and it is good to know I can now count on my new extended Thai family should I ever have a problem over here.

On our last night in the village, *Lek* suggested we have a party for her family and friends. I gave her money to go shopping and she brought back lots of food and drinks. The whole village turned up at *Lek's* house and we ran out of beer and whiskey very quickly. One of her brothers kindly drove me to a local supermarket so I could buy some more. It was an enjoyable evening and although I went to bed early, everyone else stayed up and partied until well after sunrise.

Lek's home is very primitive by our standards, Mum, and her mother and father took time to show me around. They pointed out the poor quality roof that obviously needs a lot of repair work. I can't speak Thai but *Lek* told me that when it rains the roof leaks. Her mother did not look very ill but *Lek* confided that she was simply putting on a brave front for me. Her father is very old and finds it difficult to get around. *Lek* would like to buy him a motorbike so he could ride to the market every day instead of walking.

Lek's older brother, *Somchai*, said he would come to visit us in Pattaya soon. He is *Lek's* favourite brother and they are very close. He is going to try and get a job as a motorcycle taxi driver here because there is no work for him back in the village. *Lek* said she would like him to come and stay with us until he gets on his feet. He would be good company for her when I am not around. Being very business-minded, she also suggested I buy a motorcycle so that *Somchai* can start his taxi business as soon as he arrives. He will pay me back, with interest, out of the money he earns.

For Christmas, I wanted to get *Lek* something special for being so wonderful. Even though it used up all my spare cash, I bought her the gold chain she had her little heart set on. She loved it and, as she said, it will be a good investment for both of us. She said not to worry about having no money left. To save me spending too much on her, she would return to her village for a few days until I could get more money transferred from Australia. Ever so thoughtful.

There is no shortage of great business opportunities here in Pattaya and I have made many friends, most of them publicans. It appears this is a most lucrative occupation for foreigners living in this part of Thailand. Even though they are making lots of money, many have kindly offered me partnerships in their bars. I am seriously thinking about it but there are so many offers that I don't know which one to take.

I will write again soon. Love you.
Your son.
"Kwai"

This story is
dedicated to

Pom

39

Footprints in the Sand

U p to this point I have only written about things that amuse or interest me. If it was not humourous, ironic or satirical, I really didn't want to write about it. But this story is different because, in the life-long learning process, there are twists and turns that can never be predicted. This is a story about one such twist that has been the cruelest blow of all. It begins with the belief that, because you are honest and fair with other people, they will be honest and fair to you. It begins with the feeling that you are an island and therefore immune to the 'slings and arrows of outrageous fortune'. It begins with a false notion about yourself. It begins with delusion. And what more appropriate place to be deluded than Pattaya.

What follows has been edited only in the sense of correcting grammatical and spelling errors. It may seem disjointed, convoluted, self-indulgent and emotional, but it was written as the events unfolded. My emotions changed from minute to minute so the words penned one day sometimes appear contradictory to those written the next. But I had to be honest with myself and changing any part of the story at a later date would have betrayed that honesty. It has been the most difficult story I have ever written and one that I wish I never had to. I have put my heart firmly on my sleeve and thus left myself open to ridicule and accusations of merely feeling sorry for myself. Guilty - but the story is real.

210

"The moving finger writes,
And having writ, moves on.
Nor all thy piety nor wit can lure it back to conceal half a line,
Nor all thy tears wash out a word of it."

Omar Khayyam

When I first met *Pom*, a seventeen-year-old beauty from *Lopburi*, I thought I had found someone special. She was working in a Beer Bar as cashier (genuine) and it took me three months of nightly visits to win her affection. I was told by both *Pom* and her parents, who came to Pattaya especially to meet me, that she was a virgin. They seemed to make a big deal about it but I could not have cared less. Three weeks after her eighteenth birthday, *Pom* and I moved in together.

I'm no expert but, after our first night together, I was certain that she had lied about being a virgin. Maybe she had lied to her parents as well, so I did not say anything about it. She had been to school in Bangkok and I assumed there had been a Thai boyfriend or two before me. It did not worry me and I kept my mouth shut. What did concern me was that I had caught her lying to me, on day one. I did not realize just how many more lies were to follow.

Although I did not have a lot of money, it did not seem to matter to her. There was always enough to take care of the two of us but, after two months, she began to make subtle requests for money to fix her family's 'problem'. This was no big deal because, at the time, I could afford it. I went with her to *Lopburi*, visited her home, handed over 30,000 *baht* to Mama and everyone seemed happy with that.

Once we had been together for a year, I discovered that the family's 'problem' was an annual event which she was required to address. That meant me, because I was the *fa-lung* 'son-in-law'. I was again asked to contribute 30,000 *baht* and came very close to handing it over except something was worrying me. Her attitude had changed over the past few months. She started going out alone quite a lot and I began to have some niggling suspicions. Most disturbing was that, for several months, 'Mama' had been giving *Pom* gold trinkets - a half-*baht* bracelet, then

Footprints in the Sand   A Fool In Paradise a one-*baht* necklace and then finally, a two-*baht* gold chain that she was too scared to wear around.

Considering that her mother never had more than ten *baht* to her name, I did not believe that rubbish for one second. Gold flow within a Thai family has a one-way valve. It flows from daughters to parents, not the other way round. She must have been in hysterics when she thought I fell for that bullshit! Once again, I said nothing about it but I knew she was getting the gold, or the money to buy it, from somewhere ore someone else.

My attitude began to change. She began to annoy me and I would become irritated by the slightest things. She became very moody and I did not know from one moment to the next whether she was happy or in a bad mood. I eventually laid the cards on the table and told her that I did not like the idea of taking care of her entire family as well as look after the two of us. I also made up a story that my two daughters were coming to Thailand for a holiday and I needed the money to pay their airfares. I could not give her parents the money.

Then she started. "I love you very much darling but I have to take care Mama and Papa. What can I do?" She talked with me less and less and I started to crave and yearn for the single life again. I would luxuriate in the times I could get out by myself. Then fate stepped in.

It is said that you should never trust your enemies and trust your friends even less. True words. I had known an American, Bill, for around eight months. I also knew that he liked *Pom*. She is a very attractive girl so it would have been strange if he did not like her. When we first met, he already had a girlfriend so, like a fool, I trusted him. But he had broken up with *Noi* two months earlier.

Day 1 - Thursday
Pom had been back home for a few days, presumably to tell the folks that her *fa-lung* was not going to part with any more money. She arrived back at our apartment at 11:00am. I thought this was suspicious because it takes two buses and about seven hours to get from her village

to Pattaya. That meant that she would have had to leave at 4:00am. Not likely. The afternoon spent together was 'cool' to say the least.

At some point, without saying a word, she went out only to return an hour later with her navel pierced with a stud. This was suspicious for three reasons. Number one, she had supposedly just returned from her village. How much money do Thai girls returning to Pattaya have? None. They are lucky if they escape with the bus fare. I did not give her any money so she got it from someone else. Secondly, she knew that I hate navel rings. I had told her many times that I thought they were ugly. Thirdly, my treacherous American ex-friend loved them. He had paid for his previous girlfriend, *Noi*, to have her navel pierced and I remember him telling *Pom* on many occasions that she would look beautiful with her's done as well.

She offered no explanation but that evening, dressed quickly, saying that she wanted to go to our favourite bar. No problem and we walked hand-in-hand to the bar. At around 10:00pm the American scumbag turned up alone. Nothing suspicious and not a problem. I was tired so checked bin and asked *Pom* if she was ready to leave. A resounding "No!" was her response. I spat the dummy, left alone and returned to our room. At around midnight, she arrived at the apartment, came in, grabbed something from her handbag and left without a word.

At 3:00am, I called her mobile number. After many attempts, she finally answered. She said that she had not answered before because she was at a disco and could not hear the phone. There was no noise in the background so I asked where she was now. "In Pattaya," was her answer. To cut a long story short, she finally admitted that she was in the room of 'a *fa-lung*' and was not coming home. It did not take Einstein to work out who this *fa-lung* arsehole was.

Day 2 - Friday
Pom arrived back at our apartment at 1:00pm wearing a man's shorts and man's t-shirt. Coldly, I asked her if she was coming to pick up her things. She said yes. She collected all her belongings packed in two suitcases plus a large cardboard box. When she initially moved in with

me she had a very small knapsack containing a few items of clothing and one pair of shoes. Over the past fifteen months I must have really been a bad man because she left with a *baht* bus full of clothes and shoes.

It transpires that the events of these two days were not coincidental. I found out that, some weeks (or months) earlier, the American dog had given her a key to his condo, telling her to come around any time. This low-life had been conspiring over the telephone with *Pom* before she went home to her village. The two of them had been playing me for a fool for more than two months. Remembering back over the previous few weeks, on more than one occasion I answered her mobile phone only to have the caller immediately hang up. It did not occur to me then to check the number of the caller. Lately, she also seemed to be receiving and sending an inordinant number of text messages.

As I found out later, she actually returned to Pattaya two days before coming to our apartment and spent the previous two nights with him. Perhaps she did not even go home at all. She may have spent the entire time in his condo in Naklua because she returned to our apartment with no bus ticket and her carry bag almost empty. She also did not have her toothbrush. It may seem trivial, but Thai girls are conscientious when it comes to their toothbrush. Most will carry it with them whenever there is a possibility of not returning to their room that evening. If she had innocently left her toothbrush in *Lopburi*, she would have asked me to buy her a new one. As it happened, she left it in his condo, knowing full well that she would be returning the following evening. I wrote the story 'The Toothbrush Conspiracy' and have now had the game played on me - in reverse.

What about the fact that I went to the bar with her? No problem. Perhaps their plan was that she would start a fight or say she wanted to go to a disco. She knows I hate discos and would not want to go. She would merely have insisted she go alone or with a 'friend' and I would then be out of the picture. As it happened, by leaving when I did, I made it all too easy for them. She told me later they went to a bar or disco in Naklua until it closed and then back to his nearby condo.

Day 3 - Saturday
She was gone and, following the well-thumbed Pattaya script, her
'love' lasted only as long as the money did. Why doesn't that surprise
me? When the money was not forthcoming from me, her 'love'
transferred to another bank account. In the process, I was betrayed in
the worst way by someone I thought was a friend and lost my girlfriend
as well. Double whammy.

In a scene from the movie *My Fair Lady*, Eliza, played by Audrey
Hepburn, walks out of his home and Professor Higgins, played by Rex
Harrison, sings a song basically saying that she was a pain in the neck
to live with but, now she was gone, he really missed her. "I've grown
accustomed to her face." I couldn't remember all the words but that
tune kept resounding in my head over the days to come. Her minor
annoyances seemed petty now and, in the silence of my room, lonliness
became my constant companion.

Now I was alone. But isn't that what I thought I wanted? Didn't I
want to be rid of her? My suspicions that she had been lying to me for
a long time had all proven correct so I should have been glad to see the
back of her. Unfortunately, I was about to learn something about myself
that I never knew was there. I was also to prove the old adage that you
should be careful what you wish for – it may come true.

Day 4 - Sunday
These first days after she left were not what you would call my best.
I freely admit that I was not handling it very well and discovered I was
not the 'rock' I previously thought. And the hurting did not get any
better as I followed the well-worn behavioural patterns associated with
having one's heart broken.

In my walks around the city throughout the day and night, each time
I passed a public telephone, I would call her mobile and hang up once
she answered. Now before you tell me what I already know about how
truly pathetic and juvenile that is, let me explain. At one *baht* per time,
it was very cheap therapy. Just the thought that, by answering the
telephone she was disturbed from whatever she may have been doing

and further, the hope that maybe on one or more occasion I would interrupt them during sex, brought a momentary smile to my face. And the lunatics have taken over the asylum. (An interesting statistic to come out of all this is that three out of five TOT public telephones in Pattaya don't work.)

One thing she forgot to do when she removed all her things from the apartment was to pick up the laundry. When I collected it, the bag contained two expensive pairs of jeans and six or seven of her favourite tops. Later that night, being in no frame of mind for conciliatory gestures, I sat on the floor and carefully opened the neatly-folded clothing. Then, taking out my trusty cigarette lighter, I burned the crotch out of both pairs of jeans. I put large and numerous cigarette burns through each of the tops. Becoming bored with that, into the last shirt – her favourite – I smeared a full tube of super glue. I then carefully refolded each ruined item and placed them back into the bag so that, from the outside, it appeared as if everything was fine. When and if she came to collect them, she would not notice until she unpacked them later. And I was happy.

Day 5 - Monday
Almost every long-term resident of Pattaya, both male and female, has had their heart broken at some point. In spite of prior warnings, testimonials and well-publicized accounts, it seems to go with the territory. Someone once said that "the only thing man has learned from history is that man has never learned anything from history." How true, but what the well-meaning people fail to realize is that this is not a perfect world. In a perfect world, men would listen to their peers, take account of past experiences and behave rationally, logically and reasonably. The one thing missing from the equation is 'emotion'. When the heart takes over, the first casualty is common sense.

Why is this emotion we call 'love' so powerful? Why can it begin and end so quickly? I believe what happens to a man is that even the thought of 'love', the very idea of it, triggers a chemical change in his body. Common sense goes out the window, the shutters are pulled down over reason and a sign magically appears on his forehead saying

"Nobody Home." He is blinded by the 'need' to love and to have her love him, and no price seems too high to pay.

There is the story of the guy who was married to a chronic alcoholic. She would drink herself into a stupor every night, often to the point of vomiting. She was abusive towards him, physically violent and a constant drain on his limited finances. Each time his friends tried to tell him to get rid of her, he only had one answer. "But I love her. What can I do?"

Another guy lived with his wife in a small house he owned in Pattaya. He thought that everything was going fine until he discovered that she had sold his house (worth around one million *baht*) by forging his signature on the documents. He only found out when the new owners came around to collect the 5,000 *baht* monthly rent. In the meantime the money from the proceeds of the sale was all gone and no one will ever know the truth about what happened to it. An outsider could conclude that he would be well rid of her, but no, they are still together in the same house and he is working on getting the funds to buy it back again. Is it 'love', a fear of change or simply a fear of being alone?

My own nightmare was far from over. Although I did not lose a house, car or a mountain of money, what she took from me was much more precious than that. I rode the emotional roller-coaster following the tracks of millions before me. First came the denial – "She wouldn't do that to me" - then the anger and finally the sense of loss. Basically - stupidity, irrationality and pain. The last was the worst. I felt like a guy who could walk into a dingy bar somewhere, order a bottle of whisky, a glass, a gun and three bullets. Why three bullets? Because I am so stupid I would probably miss with the first two! I began listening to old tapes of the American Country and Western singer Jim Reeves. These songs are real tear-jerkers, truly pathetic stuff. Switch on the music, fill the bath with warm water and pass me the razor blades.

Late that evening, I found myself drinking at a bar I had never been to before. Tired, emotional and with no desire to return to my room alone, I bar fined a girl in the hope she would 'help me make it through the night'. It did not work. In the morning I could not get rid of her quickly enough. I realized the only way I could bear even touching her was if I closed my eyes and pretended she was *Pom*. And with that, I became aware of something that should have been obvious to me for a long time. I loved *Pom*.

It is true that you never know what you've got until it's gone. I was in love for only the second time in my life and didn't realize it until it was too late.

Day 6 - Tuesday

So there I was – alone, miserable and hurting like hell. Today was my worst day spent in Thailand. I have been through all this before with the first woman I ever loved, my Australian ex-wife. In that case, she did get the house, the car and the kids. What was required was to sit down and remember all the mistakes I made on that occasion to ensure I did not repeat them this time. The first thing was to overcome the anger. No man can think rationally when he is filled with anger.

In the past I have found that the best way for me to do this is to walk it off. I would go out and walk anywhere and everywhere until it was out of my system. Walking also allowed me to think. After a full afternoon of pounding the pavements of Pattaya, I knew what I wanted. Two things - I wanted her back and I wanted to get revenge on the back-stabbing coward of a Yank. I hoped that by achieving the first goal, the second would automatically follow.

Pom called to ask whether I had collected the laundry and if she could come over and get it. This was my chance to assess the damage and determine if it was reversible. All I had to do was remain calm and, because I did not want her to see the depth of my pettiness, hide the clothes I had ruined. I also had to retain a 'friendly' relationship with her. If she severed all ties with me now, it would be game over.

When she arrived, she did the most annoying thing a Thai girl can do in a time of crisis - she smiled. I know this was only to cover her embarrassment but, to a Westerner, it looked as if she was very pleased with herself. I was shaking and fought to keep control. When she asked about the laundry I said that I had thrown it out in a fit of anger. She was not happy at all with that but, after accepting that I had a right to be angry, she sat down and we talked.

I had to glean as much information as possible in order to know what I was up against. Our discussion was illuminating to say the least. She tried to place the blame back on me by saying that, for the month or so prior to all this, our relationship had declined. I was angry at her family's demands for money and took it all out on her. I was less affectionate, moody and whereas I had accused her of becoming a pain in the neck, I was also.

Her family asked for thirty thousand *baht* and she asked me if I could help. I replied that I did not know. A few weeks later, she argued her parents down to twenty thousand *baht* but again I replied that I did not know. Finally, four days before she left, she sold her two-*baht* gold chain and asked if I could come up with ten thousand *baht*. I gave her the story about my daughters coming for a visit and said "No".

That was the crunch. She was under immense pressure from her family, living with a foreigner and she could not help them out with ten thousand *baht*. This was the reason she was sent to Pattaya in the first place and my refusal forced her to take the action she did. She decided that, because her family came first, she had to do something drastic. A supposedly wealthy American was her way out.

I also discovered that she had given me enough hints. She once asked, if she had to marry another man for money, how long would I wait for her. I thought she was joking and laughed it off by answering, "one year". Evidently, by saying that, my big mouth had just given her tacit approval for her plan.

But my biggest blunder was that, one night at our local bar, in a fit of unconscionable stupidity, I mouthed off to some mates that I wanted to finish with her and be single again. Of all the lunatic things I have done in my life, that has got to be the worst. The information was then relayed to the snake and I'll bet he could not tell her fast enough. When she heard, instead of confronting me with the rumour to determine whether I had actually said it and, if so, did I mean it, she decided to get in first. My big mouth again! I felt like ringing my own stupid neck.

She told me that she was no good and that I should forget her. She said that she still loved me but that with time she hoped the love would transfer to the scumbag. He was wealthy, had a nice condo, a car, was taking good care of her (financially) and had promised to help her family out with all the loot. She said he took her shopping anywhere she wanted to go, let her buy whatever she liked no matter how expensive and because of the car, she did not have to walk anywhere or catch *baht* taxis. Shit, if I had known she hated walking so much, I would have bought her a pair of roller skates!

The cards were out on the table. Before she left, we fell into each other's arms, kissing passionately and tearfully. She promised to keep in touch and come and see me when she could.

After she left, I felt better. Even though in the back of my mind I realized she probably only told me what she thought I wanted to hear, my assessment was that it wasn't over yet and there was a slim chance I could still get her back. This intelligence now gathered, I needed to formulate a plan. At the moment, the low-life had all the advantages. He was throwing his money at her and that was something against which I could not compete. Nor did I want to. He was also with her constantly so could keep her attention focussed on him.

I regained a little self-respect with the truth that I had won her heart whereas he was simply attempting to buy it with hard currency. And what sort of pathetic excuse for a human being is he? In a town with thousands of available women, he has to chase after someone else's girlfriend - someone he pretented to befriend as well. Where I come from, that is the act of a dog. He has no respect or consideration for anyone and I feel sorry for any guy who is under the mistaken belief that he is a 'friend'. Once he tires of *Pom* or she dumps him, he will do the same thing to someone else. Like a scorpion, it's in his nature.

220

Day 7 - Wednesday

I spent the day alone, making and receiving no phonecalls. Flicking through my Thai-English dictionary, I came across a photo wedged between the pages. It was of the two of us and taken a few weeks earlier. On the back, *Pom* had written in English, 'I love you, but.' The 'but' was double underlined. That said it all, really. I cursed the fact that I had not found it before but, if I had, would I have fully understood it and therefore, would it have made a difference?

Day 8 - Thursday

She phoned and we arranged to meet at my apartment. It was an excellent chance to ascertain if my plan was working. She lied to him about where she was going and that was one string to my bow. When she arrived about thirty minutes later, we talked for a while – and then we made love. It was fantastic. Here was a girl who had left me for someone else and she was back making love with me. Afterwards, we lay in each other's arms and talked.

We came to an arrangement. She promised to keep in touch every day and come to see me as often as she could. She asked me to be patient and just think of her as 'going to work'. I agreed but knew it would be difficult. She promised to dump him and come back with me as soon as the family's 'problem' was fixed. Foolishly, I believed her.

I was hoping cracks would start appearing in their relationship. She did have expensive tastes – an option she could not exercise while she stayed with me. Once he realized just how much money she could spend, he may get annoyed. She can also be very moody and hot-headed. I remembered him telling me once that these were qualities he did not appreciate in a woman.

He, on the other hand, is self-centred, boorish and arrogant - the archetypal 'Ugly American'. This would eventually grate on her. She was also starting to miss our mutual friends who they could not visit as a couple in case I was there. Almost everyone *Pom* knew in Pattaya she met through me and the Yank coward would not dare show his ugly face at the places we used to frequent. She could talk to her friends over the telephone, but was lonely. Most importantly, we now had a secret - a secret which I would reveal to the usurper at the appropriate time.

All I needed to do was keep the pressure on, keep the train rolling and wait. But that is easier said than done. The ache and loneliness in my heart was chronic and not a minute went by that I did not think about her. We kept in touch by sending text messages to each other but, not speaking with her was too much to bear. I would call her and speak in Thai. She would tell me how much she loved and missed me. I did not care if he knew it was me on the line but I understood her desire to protect herself. At the same time, if he suspected that all these phone calls and messages were from me, asked her about them and she lied to him, the cracks would widen. If she told him the truth, it would annoy him and the cracks would still widen. Either way, it would be a good result. I had to keep a wedge between them to cover my greatest fear – that she would eventually fall in love with him or, at least, his money.

On Monday she was going to go back home for three days and I suggested that she tell him it would be for five days and she could stay with me for the last two. Her agreement was particularly satisfying as it meant I would be doing exactly the same to him that he had done to me. The prospect of revenge was getting sweeter. When the time was right, I would simply let one of his few remaining friends know what had been going on behind his back and, hopefully, he would finish with her. My optimism knew no bounds.

Day 9 - Friday
She sent me a text message in the morning saying she loved me but by mid-afternoon I was frantic. I thought that surely she would have been able to find the time alone to call and talk to me. I called her from a public phone. When she answered and discovered it was me, she hung up. I did not understand. On the one hand she kept telling me she loved me and yet she did not want to talk to me. If she was afraid he would hear her conversation, she could have spoken Thai and pretended she was talking to a girlfriend. She was good at that because I was certain that was what she had been doing to me for some time.

I was frantic and, in desperation, called a friend to ask his wife to talk with her and find out once and for all if what she had been telling me was the truth. The first call, the phone rang out so we waited for *Pom* to call back. Eventually she did. The essence of the conversation was that she did not love the Yank - yet. My friend knew this to be true. I was told that as soon as she got time alone, she would call me. Maybe that night or the following day. The waiting was horrific.

That night delivered another cruel blow. I went to my usual watering hole and, in my severely depressed state, talked with the cashier who was one of my girlfriend's close friends and confidants. She told me what I did not want to hear. She confirmed my suspicion that *Pom* had actually come back two days early from her village and slept with the American bastard for the two nights before she left me. It is one thing to suspect something based on circumstantial evidence, but to then have it confirmed comes as a devastating blow. That arsehole sat, drank and joked with me while, all the time, he had been screwing my girlfriend for at least the previous two nights. Maybe they had been seeing and screwing each other for much longer than that. When I had confronted her with my suspicion, she naturally denied everything.

What was I to believe? The strange thing is, I knew if she came back to me, I could forget everything she had done or lied about. I was single-minded and cared about nothing else. Time to reassess my position. This began badly and just went downhill from there.

I knew where he lived so why didn't I just go around there and beat the living shit out of him? As satisfying as that would be, it could backfire badly. It could push them closer together and suddenly I would be the bad guy. I would have to be patient. His time will come.

From the other perspective, there would be nothing he could do to make her leave him, not as long as the money kept rolling in for her family. He could screw around, treat her badly or abuse her and she would still stay. The only way was for him to dump her, but it had to happen soon. The problem was there was no guarantee that, even if he threw her out, she would come back to me. She may get used to the high life and not want to return to the austere life that I could offer. She may go looking for another rich *fa-lung*. As I fell asleep, I recognized that the odds were well and truly stacked against me and, deep down, knew I would never get her back.

Day 10 - Saturday
Waking early, I realized the situation could not go on the way things were and today would be major decision time. If she called and arranged to meet me secretly, perhaps my confidence that we would eventually be reunited would be restored. If she did not call by midday, I would keep phoning her until she spoke to me.

My feelings were becoming ambivalent. I now did not know whether the force that kept me going was the desire to have her back or merely the desire to break them up and not let him win. She left me for him because he could provide the material wealth she sought and keep her in a style I never could. She was now leading the life she always wanted to lead. But they had committed the ultimate betrayal and, in my mind, deserved to be punished. I thought I could forgive her but became determined to take any opportunity to make his life as miserable as possible, the same as he had made mine.

I had the evidence of the text messages she sent me over the last few days but those alone were not enough. My only real weapon was the day we made love. I was certain he did not know about it and was hoping that, when he found out, he would be furious at her. Even if he forgave her, it would leave him always suspicious and his jealousy may eventually get too much for her. Jealousy is a cumulative emotion, it never diminishes. Once the seeds of suspicion are planted, they never die.

I needed at least one more time with her to make it work. If that was not possible, the following Monday was my deadline because I would pass the information on to our only remaining mutual friend and let him inform the Yank maggot. I was a drowning man and it was fast becoming my only straw. Still, he could not be with her all the time. She had to get some moments alone. He played golf two days a week but the better news was that he was going to return to America for a few weeks at the end of the month. She would be able to talk freely with me then. I was hoping against hope that she would also want to see me.

Twelve o'clock came and she had not called. Not willing to wait any longer, I called her. When she finally answered, she was very evasive in answering my questions but that could have been because the Yank arsehole was there. She said she had not called because the card in her telephone had run out. I did not believe that for a second. When I asked if we still had our arrangement, she said yes. When I asked if she still loved me, she said yes. When I asked if she still wanted to get back together with me, she said yes.

The effect of the phone call was it showed that at least she was willing to talk with me. This time, she did not cancel the call once she saw my number come up on the display. The down side was she simply told me what she knew I wanted to hear. But why would she want to keep feeding me a load of bullshit? Why not just tell me to piss off and be done with it? At the time I was even more confused but, a few months down the track, I came to understand what she was up to.

Later that afternoon I ran into a good friend of mine who kindly loaned me his shoulder to cry on and his ear to bombard. He listened patiently and then, like a true friend should, he let me have it.

"You wrote the book *Money Number One*. Go home and read it! You said it yourself many times – do you really think the gorgeous, young girls hanging off the arms of the decrepit old men walking around Pattaya are there because they are in love with these guys? Neil, you are old, fat and ugly and *Pom* has left you for a creep ten years older and ten times uglier than you. Why did she do that? Is she simply attracted to old men - the more pathetic, the better - or could it be something else? I'll give you a hint – it starts with 'M', has five letters and rhymes with 'honey' - and if this unctuous arsehole thinks she has gone with him for any other reason, he is a bigger fool than you are!"

Then he told me something which made even more sense.

"What are you complaining about? Didn't you once tell me that you were getting sick of her? Think of it this way - you have found out two very important things: Firstly, he is a lying, back-stabbing snake with more faces than a Taiwanese watch factory and not worthy of your friendship nor anybody else's for that matter. Secondly, she is a lying, cheating, money-grabbing whore who is not worthy of your affection, let alone your love. Isn't it better that you found out now rather than in one or two years time? They've done you a favour!"

He did not have to be so brutal, but he was one hundred percent correct.

At 7:00pm I went to my local bar and asked *Pom's* cashier friend to call *Pom* and let me speak with her. She called, had a brief conversation, then handed me the phone. *Pom's* mood was no longer conciliatory. She told me not to call her any more, she did not want to see me any more and it was definitely over. Then she hung up. For the first time, I was hearing the truth.

Day 11 - Sunday
I awoke and read *Money Number One*, beginning with the chapter entitled 'The *Fa-lung* In Love'. That chapter was like a diary of the events that had just unfolded. I started to laugh at the irony of reading *me* telling *me* not to do all the things I just did. I had not listened to one piece of my own advice. I did buy her a mobile phone and it was eventually used against me. I did trust her, or at least, overlook her lies, and it was eventually used against me. I did not move her away from the temptations of Pattaya and it was eventually used against me. Finally, I completely underestimated the level of influence her family had over her, her blind loyalty to them and thus the lengths she would go to in order to help them. I had written that the *fa-lung* boyfriend or husband is Number 13 on a Thai girl's list of priorities and had just confirmed it.

Reflection
To sum up, the pinguid Yank has purchased himself a girlfriend. He did not win her affection as I had done, he merely paid money for her. He bought himself a beautiful, raven-haired Barbie Doll that he can

dress up, attach to his arm and parade around. A friend and I did some quick calculations. With her new gold bracelet, new gold chain, original designer label wardrobe, two trips home to visit the family, the 10,000 *baht* she bragged about having in her new bank account and, assuming he handed over the 30,000 *baht* to temporarily alleviate her family's 'problem', he would not have seen much change out of 100,000 *baht*. That is in less than a month! She was an expensive purchase.

In the process he has been exposed as the total reptile he is and has lost many friends over it. He has shown he is totally untrustworthy and capable of any dispicable act. As I said before, where I come from, stealing a mate's girlfriend is the act of a dog. Any of his current acquaintences should be very wary of leaving their own girlfriend alone in a room with him, especially if she is young and gorgeous.

Maybe he feels it was worth it. The test will come when she finally has all the money to satisfy her family's immediate needs or if his money runs out in the meantime. I don't care how rich he told her he was, he will not be able to sustain that type of expenditure and, once the 'honeymoon' is over, *Pom's* fall back to reality will be severe.

Her parents have achieved exactly what they wanted – their daughter attached to a *fa-lung* with money. That is why they sent her to Pattaya in the first place and my intervention merely delayed the inevitable. I was a 'short time' that simply lasted fifteen months too long. They will now have their immediate financial problems attended to and be very happy. It will be interesting to know if, or when, they come up with more financial woes for their daughter's new companion to solve. If he marries her, they are in for another windfall. *Pom* once mentioned to me that, when she married, her parents required that the groom cough up 200,000 *baht* in cash plus 10 *baht* in gold!

Pom also has what she wanted. She has been bought and paid for and now has the money to do anything, go anywhere and buy anything she wants. She now travels around the city in a car, rather than by *baht* bus. She no longer has to gaze with envy at the other Thai ladies in Pattaya who have rich *fa-lung* boyfriends or husbands.

As I said at the beginning of this story, it all begins with delusion. Deluding yourself to believe that this place is about anything other than money. As for me, hindsight is a wonderful thing. What man alive would not trade a megaton of hindsight for a milligram of foresight? Months before her inglorious departure, the signs were there. If only I had not overlooked the lies I knew she was telling me. If only I had paid a little more attention to the signs, I would not be in such a mess now. If only I had recognized the lengths she would go to in order to fix her family's financial problems. If only ...

Many well-meaning people have told me that I am well rid of her. I could accept that apart from one important factor - living without her is a nightmare. I have joined the exploding ranks of the broken-hearted men who would do anything to have their errant partner back. Although I don't fully understand why, I can finally empathize with their feelings.

There are two positive things to come out of this mess. The first is the knowledge that all I have written about in the past, all that I suspected, all my theories and conjectures have been confirmed. The second is that I know a lot more about myself. Maybe my story will help some other poor bastard in the future. If not, then at least writing it has helped me. I cling to the belief that their relationship, based purely on his lust and her greed, will not endure. 'Love' does not enter the equation. He has exposed his true nature and she her's so, unless I have missed something, their chances don't look good.

Two Weeks Later
I received one phonecall from *Pom* asking me why I was no longer speaking with our cashier friend from the bar. She must have called *Pom* and told her that I was angry with her. This was my chance to use some psychology. I replied that I was angry with her because the girl had lied to me by saying that, before our breakup, *Pom* had already spent at least two nights with the insipid Yank, whereas *Pom* had told me she had not.
"You say you not lie, so she must have lied to me. Which one of you is lying?"
After a brief silence, her answer came back.

"Maybe me."

"What do you mean, 'maybe me'? Either you lied or she did."

"Maybe I lie."

Her answer never changed from that.

I swear I am going to travel throughout this country on a purchasing mission. I am looking to buy - and will pay big money for - a straight answer. All I want, from just one Thai, is a straight, truthful answer to any simple question. Yes or no. Black or white. I have a feeling I would be more successful joining John Cleese and Eric Idle in seeking the Holy Grail. Thailand must have the only judicial system in the world where the Bailiff asks the defendant, "How do you plead - guilty, not guilty or maybe?"

The young, sweet, affectionate girl I loved and who, I believed, did love me in her own Thai way, no longer exists. She may still be living in Pattaya but she has been replaced by a greedy, self-centred snob who lies to her family, friends and boyfriends. That girl I don't want to know. The only love she appears to have in her heart now is the love of money and the high life, which I predict, will ultimately be her downfall. In that respect, they make a perfect couple. Only time will tell.

It has taken almost four weeks for me to finally achieve 'closure' on our relationship. It came unexpectedly when she informed me that she had his name tattooed below her bikini line. She is a very slim girl so I wondered how the tattooist got the words 'A Piece of Shit' to fit. That did it for me. She was with me for fifteen months and not once did I ask her to disfigure her beautiful body. She was living with him less than three weeks and had her navel pierced, her pubic hair shaved and a tattoo of his cowardly name permanently polluting her lovely skin.

What next? A nose ring? Breast implants? Skin bleaching treatment? Hair dyed blonde? He has stolen one of Thailand's most beautiful girls and, like a piece of clay, is moulding her into some adolescent fantasy of his own. Nature made her the way she was and he is systematically disfiguring her.

But, how mentally defective and insecure must a man be to ask his girlfriend to indelibly disfigure her body with a tattoo of his name? Is it his way of saying that she is now 'his' property? And how stupid is she to comply? He is three times her age, for God's sake. Does she really think he is going to out-live her? Sooner or later, he will be out of the picture but she will wear that offensive graffiti forever. I was amused by the thought that, if his name was indeed tattooed below her bikini line as she had indicated, it was appropriately positioned.

In times of trouble, people learn who their true friends are and, I am happy to say, these events have enabled me to separate the chaff from the wheat. All but two of the guys who knew the parties involved supported, encouraged and helped me get through it. Without them, I could not have done it. To the two who didn't help me, you were no real loss. I have severed contact with all the Thai girls involved because, I am convinced, they all knew what was going on behind my back. I am also certain that a few of them actively encouraged *Pom*'s deception while smiling and pretending to be my 'best' friends.

News Flash!!!

Five months have now passed and there have been some developments. I'm not going to say how I found out, suffice to say that Pattaya is a very small town and I know quite a few people.

It appears that little miss innocent, *Pom*, was not so innocent after all. I had always believed the picture she portrayed as being young, naïve and under intense pressure from her parents to come up with some loot. Since I was not handing it over, she was firmly between a rock and a hard place and was forced to do what she did. Not so! According to my source, she had been fucking that American piece of garbage for EIGHT MONTHS before her ignominious departure from my life. That would mean their affair began around May-June 2002 which would have been around the time I first met him and introduced the two of them - and while he was still living with *Noi*. *Pom* and *Noi* appeared to be friends but I remember her commenting that *Noi* always dressed sexy and wore lots of gold. She was envious.

She had the opportunity every time I went out alone and I do recall that she refused to go with me some times saying that she didn't like going to that particular place. I knew the reason the craven coward and *Noi* broke up was because of *Pom*, but had assumed that it was because *Noi* suspected that he lusted after her. Another person informed me recently that the reason *Noi* left him was because she had actually come back to the condo unexpectedly and caught him in bed with another woman. It is highly likely, in the light of the new information, that *Noi* actually caught him in bed with *Pom*! I remember the last time I saw *Noi* together with the sewer rat at around Christmas time, she ignored me and refused to talk to *Pom*. Prior to that, they used to phone each other and chat all the time. I am only guessing but, I would not be surprised to learn that the cunning *Pom* purposefully 'allowed' *Noi* to find out about their liaison. That would not have been difficult for her to do.

Another interesting piece of information is that the Yank animal is not as rich as he makes out or, should I say, *Pom* makes out. This also fits. Yes, he has a car and rents a nice condo, but has not much else. I remember him telling me once that he "needed to make some money" and someone told me a few weeks ago that they were looking for a new place to live. I cannot believe that he would be looking for a better place. Instead, I think they are looking for a 'cheaper' place, which will not please the social-climbing *Pom* at all.

Pom had been bragging to everyone, including one girl who I had always assumed was her number one friend and who she treated as her 'big sister', that he is mega-rich and gives her 40,000 to 50,000 *baht* per month. Money is no object, she said. Not so, according to my source. He only gives her 10,000 *baht* per month. This is consistent with what I already knew. Shortly after she ran off, she boasted to me about opening a new bank account. When I asked her how much the pond scum gave her to put in it, she replied 10,000 *baht*. Coincidence?

So, apparently, all is not the bed of roses *Pom* expected it to be and putting up with a geriatric, boring, fat, grotesquely ugly American with no redeeming features, no friends and not that much money is no fun. *Pom* laughed with a friend that, once or twice a week, sex consists of him popping two Viagra in an attempt to encourage his miniscule and dysfunctional equipment into some semblance of activity, while she quaffs six Heineken and sits counting money in an attempt to make him appear even remotely attractive. A union made in heaven.

Finally, my source told me that from the moment she met the Yank bastard, *Pom* was seduced by his lifestyle and the money she thought he had. I find it difficult to understand because there are still some unanswered questions. If so, why did she stay with me for so long and why, after she forced *Noi* out of the picture, did she stay with me for another two months?

I can only conclude that she was waiting for one final *baht*-fix from me, presumably the family's annual 30,000 *baht* 'problem' (due in March). I'm now convinced that, if I had handed over the money, she would STILL have done what she did. An even more sinister thought is that *he* was the puppeteer and told her to wait until she got the money from me in order to save himself the cash. Nothing would surprise me about that bastard.

Secondly, after being gone for more than six weeks, why did she call me and cry over the phone saying that she missed me, still loved me and wanted me to wait for her. Obviously she realized that the grass was not as green as she thought it was and wanted to keep the option of returning to me open.

Would you believe that finding all this out has actually been a relief? The weight of a thousand elephants has been lifted from my shoulders and, in spite of being treated like an idiot for fifteen months by a nineteen-year-old whore from *Lopburi*, it could have been a lot worse. Thankfully, I had the sense to listen to that little voice inside telling me that it smelled a rat. Imagine how I would have felt if I had handed over the 30,000 *baht* and she left me the following day?

With most of the pieces to the puzzle in place, I was tempted to make a few adjustments to my 'love story' but eventually decided to leave everything as written to serve as an example of how a middle-aged man can get caught up in an emotional upheaval. As for *Pom* and that unctuous piece of manure, they deserve each other. Together, they have destroyed two relationships, broken many friendships and shown their true colours to everyone. Do you think they care? Not a chance.

But living with someone is not as exciting as having an affair with them, so nature will take its course. They both have the morals of a sewer rat and eventually, they will do unto each other as they have done unto others. *When* it happens, I will find out about it and Eskimos in Alaska will hear my laughter. "He who laughs last ..."

Six months later, new information has come to light. Through my reliable sources, I have heard that the love-match of a lifetime has begun the rocky slide to disaster. The signs were already there that Daddy-Big-Bucks Yank was not as wealthy as he made out and *Pom* was forced to exaggerate (lie about) her wonderful new lifestyle to her friends in order to save face and hide the fact that she realized she had made one huge blunder. It now appears that his financial woes are much greater than even she imagined. He has reduced her monthly 'salary' to 5,000 *baht*, a move with which *Pom* is none too happy. She has started to badmouth him to her Thai friends and whereas she once described their first month together as like being on 'honeymoon', she now knows the honeymoon is over.

Another friend ran into them in *Sri Racha* and relayed information back to me that *Pom* confessed she was no longer happy and was basically getting sick and tired of him. All he has to do now is move to a cheaper apartment, sell his car or her gold in order to pay some bills and she will be off like a bride's nightie. If he returns to America to try and secure more funds, while the Fat Cat is away, she is one little mouse who is going to play!

From *Pom*'s point of view, what are her options? She has destroyed any chance she ever had of marrying a respectable Thai man. Her initial career choice of working in a bar, her decision to live with two *fa-lung* in succession and the fact she has the putrid name of the current one tattooed near her money-making asset will not endear her to Thai men - at least the ones with any money. Once she finishes with the current cretin, she is unlikely to return home to mama and papa to look for a respectable job in *Lopburi*. There is no money in that.

Therefore she is stuck with going with *fa-lung* and would have to stay near the tourist and bar areas frequented by foreigners. She certainly has the body to enable her to make big money by working in a Go Go Bar but again, she has that offensive tattoo. Unless she finds a victim with the same poxy name, she is unlikely to last more than 'short-time' with any one customer. As well as that, after the high life she has been leading for the past two years, returning to bar work would be a loss of face.

Her only recourse and indeed, the only game she is good at, is to jump out of the bed of one *fa-lung* and straight into the bed of the next pigeon. No break. That is what she did with me and I'm certain she has the same plans for the half-wit Yank. In fact, I heard from a totally unexpected but impeccably reliable source that she has already started. She is pissed off with the moron, has already cheated on him and is currently grooming his replacement. What a girl! My joy knows no bounds and I am rehearsing my "*som num* fucking *nah*" speech.

In terms of my lifetime, this incident is no more significant than footprints in the sand. A wave of truth has erased the impressions and any modicum of guilt I may have harboured that it was in some way my fault or that I could have done something to change the eventual outcome, is gone. To prove it, I ask myself the all-important question: If she wanted to come back to me, would I take her back? The answer is a resounding, "Not even if she came crawling on her pierced belly!"

APPENDIX

Glossary Of Terms

a-roi	Thai for 'delicious' (relating to food)
baht	Unit of Thai Currency. At the time of writing, the exchange rate was roughly forty-four Thai *baht* to the US dollar. Also a measurement of the weight of gold. One *'baht'* of Thai gold weighs just over fifteen grams and will cost between six thousand and eight thousand Thai *baht* depending on the current world price of gold.
bin	Directly translated as 'bill'. Used to describe your invoice, account or the wooden or plastic cup in which the individual drink or food invoices are placed.
boomsing	Thai slang for 'sex' or the sex act. Probably originated from German slang.
Cheap Charlie	A miser, a skinflint. Someone who does not spend a lot of money.
Check Bin	To pay your bill at a bar or restaurant.
fa-lung	Any non-Thai person, although most often used when referring to a person of Caucasian (European) appearance. Usually written as *'farang'*.
gin kao	To have a meal (literally - to eat rice)
horng nahm	Thai for bathroom or toilet (literally - room water)

Jomtien Beach	The beach resort immediately south of Pattaya Bay..
kamoyee	Thai verb meaning 'to steal'.
mai mee bun hah	Thai for 'no problem'.
mai pairng	Thai for 'not expensive'.
mai roo	Thai for 'I don't know (something)'.
mai roo-juk	Thai for 'I don't know (recognize)' someone or something.
mai sabai	Thai for 'unwell' or 'feeling sick'.
Mamasan	Sometimes written as *Mamasang*. She is the 'madam' or bar manager overseeing the day to day operations of the bar and keeping the girls in line.
mia noi	Thai for a 'minor (second) wife'.
Naklua	The township immediately north of Pattaya Bay.
nit noy	Thai for 'a little bit'.
pinguid	English word meaning 'fat, oily'.
pun hah baht	1,500 *baht*.
ray-o	Thai for 'fast, quickly'.
'Ring the bell'	Most bars have a large bell hanging prominently somewhere. If a customer 'rings the bell' it means he is buying a drink for everyone in the bar, both customers and staff.
sanook	Thai for 'fun'.
satang	Unit of Thai Currency, with one hundred *satang* to the *baht*. There are only two coin denominations, twenty-five *satang* and fifty *satang* and they are only used in supermarkets and department stores.
sawatdee	Thai greeting, like saying hello.
Sick Buffalo Story	Euphemism for any tale of woe told by a bar girl to a *fa-lung* in order to extract money from him. Not so much nowadays, but the girls used to tell boyfriends that the family buffalo was sick and she needed money for medicine or vet bills.
som num nah	Thai for 'it serves you right' or 'you deserved it'.
soo-ay	Thai for 'beautiful'.
tee-ruk	Thai for 'darling'.
tuk-tuk	Three-wheeled mini taxi used throughout Thailand but not in Pattaya.

BILL	PAUL	IAN
D 10	A	C 7
C 7	C 7	B 3
D 10	A	C 7
C 7	A	D 10
C 7	A	C 7
D 10	B 3	D 10
B 3	C 7	B 3
D 10	B 3	B 3
D 10	C 7	D 10
D 10	B 3	D 10
(84)	(23)	(21)